JUNOT'S INVASION
OF
PORTUGAL

JUNOT'S INVASION OF PORTUGAL

(1807-1808)

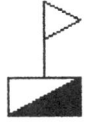

WORLEY PUBLICATIONS
2000
with Brigade Library

Facimile Edition Published 2000
by Worley Publications
10, Rectory Road East
Felling
Tyne and Wear
NE10 9DN
Telephone (0191) 469 2414

Published from the 1829 edition

This Edition © Worley Publications

ISBN 1 86980453 8

Printed and Bound in Great Britain by Anthony Rowe Ltd.
Bumper's Farm, Chippenham, Wiltshire.

BOOK I.

In the course of the month of August, in the year 1807, an army of twenty-five thousand men was assembled at Bayonne. It was called the Corps of Observation of the Gironde. Under this modest name, and with this defensive semblance, the French troops had once before, in 1801, crossed the Pyrenees, traversed Spain, and imposed a burthensome capitulation on Portugal. The Gironde Corps of Observation was not formed at the expense of the French armies of Germany, Poland, or Italy. It was made up of troops which had been left in the interior to guard the Norman and Breton coasts; namely, the seventieth and eighty-sixth regiments of infantry, two regiments which, not having been engaged in the last campaigns of the Emperor, contained a great number of old soldiers; several third battalions, which were composed only of raw troops; Swiss battalions; and two legions, one of Piedmontese, the other of Hanoverians. The battalions were from a thousand to twelve hundred strong. The cavalry consisted of fourth squadrons, supplied by the conscription of the current year, and embodied in temporary regiments. In this organisation, the men, the horses, the dresses, the equipments, every thing was new, except the officers, non-commissioned officers, and four horsemen in each company, who were the only persons that had seen actual service. Fifty pieces of field-artillery were assigned to this army. As the battalions of the artillery train were all employed on foreign service, the Government, in order to provide draught-horses, had recourse to a contractor, whom it entrusted with soldiers, and who engaged to supply horses furnished with all that was necessary to take the field.

France had no longer an enemy on the Continent, yet an army was assembling at the foot of the Pyrenees. If there could have been any doubt in the public mind as to the destination of this army, it must have been removed on hearing the name of the general to whom the Emperor had confided the command.

In the first war of the Revolution, the colonel of artillery, Bonaparte, was constructing a battery before Toulon, which treason had put into the hands of foreign armies. Having occasion to give on the ground orders which could not be transmitted verbally, a young serjeant, of the second battalion of the Côte d'Or, came forward to write from his dictation. The ships and bomb-vessels of the English and Spaniards, crowded in the lesser road of Toulon, kept up a heavy fire, to retard the establishing of the battery. A bomb fell near enough to Bonaparte and his secretary to cover them with earth and gravel. "That 's just the thing," said the latter, turning the page; "I wanted some sand to dry my paper." Bonaparte asked him his name. It was Junot. He had received a liberal education. After the capture of Toulon, Bonaparte was raised to the rank of brigadier-

THE ARMY OF PORTUGAL
Junot DUKE OF ABRANTES General in Chief.
Thiebault, General of Brigade, Chief of Staff.
Taviel, General of Brigade, Commandant of Artillery
Vincent, Colonel, Commandant of Engineers.
Quesnel, General of Division, Govenor of Oporto.
Solignac, General of Brigade, Commandant of Cascàes.

FIRST DIVISION
Comte Delaborde, General of Division.
Avril, General of Brigade.
Baron Brenier, General of Brigade.

Colonel De La Chatre	47th Line (2nd Bat.)	1.210
Colonel Rouyer	70th Line (1st & 2nd Bats.)	2.299
Chef de Bat. Felbert	4th Swiss (1st Bat.)	1.190
Chef de Bat. Recouvreur	15th Line (3rd Bat.)	1.033
Colonel Lacroix	86th Line (1st & 2nd Bats)	2.116
	7 Battalions	7.908

SECOND DIVISION

Loison, General of Division.
Charlaud, General of brigade
Baron Thomieres, General of Brigade.

Major Meslier	2nd Light (3rd Bat.)	1.255
	4th Light (3rd Bat.)	1.196
Major Petit	12th Light (3rd Bat.)	1.302
	15th Light (3rd Bat.)	1.314
Major Bertrand	32nd Line (3rd Bat.)	1.265
	58th Line (3rd Bat.)	1.394
Colonel Segeesser	2nd Swiss (2nd Bat.)	755
	7 Battalions	8.481

JUNOT'S INVASION

THIRD DIVISION

Baron Travot, General of Division. Commandant.
Fusier, General of Brigade
Graindorge, General of Brigade

Major Durlong	31st Light (3rd Bat.)	653
	32nd Light (3rd Bat.)	983
Chef de Bataillon Dien	26th Line (2nd Bat.)	537
Colonel Maransin	Legion du Midi	
	(1st & 2nd Bats)	797
Chef de Bat. Creste	66th Line (3rd & 4th Bats.)	1.004
Chef de Bat. Petavy	82nd Line (3rd Bat)	861
Colonel Striffler	Hanoverian Legion	703
	8 Battalions	5.538

CAVALRY DIVISION

Comte Kellermann, General of Division
Baron Margaron, General of Brigade
Baron Maurin, General of Brigade

Major Weiss	26th Chasseurs (4th Sq.)	244
Major Contant	1st Dragoons (4th Sq.)	261
	3rd Dragoons (4th Sq.)	236
MajorTheron	4th Dragoons (4th Sq.)	262
	5th Dragoons (4th Sq.)	249
Major Leclerc	9th Dragoons (4th Sq.)	257
	15th Dragoons (4th Sq.)	245
	7 Squadrons	1.754

OF PORTUGAL

GENDARMERIE

Chef d'escadron Thomas   Gendarmes à Cheval   38

ARTILLERY & ENGINEERS

Baron Taviel, General of Brigade.Commandant
Colonel Prost, Chief of Staff
Colonel Douence,Chief of Artillery Reserve
Colonel Foy
Colonel D'aboville
Colonel Piccot

1st Regiment à Pied	4th Comp.	112
3rd Regiment à Pied	8th & 12th Comps.	336
6th Regiment à Pied	15th & 16th Comps.	222
D'ouvriers'	9th Comp.	30
	38 Guns	700

Captain Veron	12th Bat. Artillery Train	373
Captain Francois	8th Bat.Train des Equipages	303

Colonel Vincent,Chief of Engineers
Chef de Bataillon Bruley,Chief of Staff
Chef de Bataillon Girod de Novillars

Captains, No: 11, Lieutenants, No: 2...Troups du Genie   18

Chirurgien en Chef Beaumarchef
Medecen en Chef Maillard
Pharmacien en Chef Paulet

general. Junot, whom he made his aid-de-camp, fought, prospered, and grew great, by the side of the man with whom he first became acquainted amidst the shower of shot and shells. Colonel-general of hussars, grand-officer of the empire, governor of Paris, he was likewise aid-de-camp of the Emperor Napoleon, and he was much prouder of that title than of all his other employments and dignities.

In the beginning of 1805, Junot was sent ambassador to Portugal: but a few months, however, elapsed subsequent to his arrival at Lisbon, when war broke out between Austria and France. The aid-de-camp ambassador asked and obtained permission to quit for a time his pacific mission, and flew to resume his warlike occupation. He travelled seven hundred leagues in less than twenty days, and was fortunate enough to reach the bivouac of Austerlitz the night before the battle. After the peace of Presburg he did not return to Portugal, though he continued to be ambassador to the Court of Lisbon. The Emperor nomminated General Junot to the command-in-chief of the Corps of Observation of the Gironde, and placed at the head of his staff Brigadier-general Thiebault, author of some valuable works on the service of the general and divisional staffs.

Junot joined the army early in the month of September, and reviewed the troops. The first division of infantry, under General Delaborde, was at Bayonne. The second division, which was to be led by General Loison, occupied St. Jean de Luz and the neighbouring villages on the Spanish frontier. The corps composing the third division, under General Travot, arrived at Navarreins and St. Jean de Pied de Port. The cavalry, commanded by the general of division, Kellerman, was cantoned on the Gaves, towards Pau and Oleron, and on the Adour, towards Aire and Castelnau. The general-officers and the commanders of corps disciplined the young soldiers, exercised the old, and were actively engaged in collecting the means of marching and of fighting. The artillery, which was under the direction of Brigadier-general Taviel, was brought into order, and rendered fit for rapid service. Colonel Vincent who was the superintendent of engineers at Bayonne was attached to the army, together with other officers of his corps, drawn from the garrisons of this frontier. Trousset, the intendant-commissary, was made commissary-in-chief. No magazines, or convoys of provisions were formed, but a train of military equipages, and a certain number of military commissaries were appointed to march with the troops, to establish an administrative system when the proper time should arrive. Merchants, the major part of them of that class of speculators who carry on commerce with more industry than capital, flocked from all quarters, to follow an army destined to invade the country of diamonds and of gold.

While the titular ambassador from the Emperor of the French to the Prince Regent of Portugal was getting every thing in readiness at Bayonne for a military aggression upon that kingdom, the chief secretary of the embassy, M. de Rayneval, who was chargé-d'affaires in his absence, began the diplomatic attack at Lisbon. On the 12th of August he delivered to the Portuguese government the injunction to declare immediate war against England, to confiscate English property, and to arrest, as hostages, such British subjects as were settled in Portugal.* The Count del Campo-de-Alange, ambassador from the King of Spain, presented at the same time a note, which, though less imperative in its manner, was equally threatening in its matter. The representatives of the two great powers declared, that, in the event of the Court of Portugal refusing to enter heartily and thoroughly into the Continental league against the oppressors of the sea, they had orders to demand their passports, and to depart, after having declared war.

In reply to the notes transmitted to his minister of the foreign department, the Prince Regent declared, that, to gratify his powerful allies, the Emperor of France and the King of Spain, he was ready to exclude the ships of Great Britain from his ports; but that the moderation of his government, and his religions principles, would not suffer him to adopt such a rigorous and unjust measure, in the midst of peace, as the confiscation of English property, and the imprisonment of merchants, who had nothing to do with political affairs, and resided in the country under the guarantee of his royal word.

This reply had been settled in concert with England, and it also expressed the personal opinions of the Prince. Emigration to Brazil was a thing quite repugnant to his indolent habits. Preparations for that step were at that moment actually making, not, indeed, without his knowledge, but in consequence of resolutions which originated with others, and not with him. His will, if he had had energy enough to express any, would have been, to continue to live peaceably and piously in his monastic palace of Mafra. He would have thought no sacrifice too great, to resolve the insoluble problem of giving satisfaction to both England and France.

On the 30th of September, the French chargé-d'affaires and the Spanish ambassador quitted Lisbon. The inhabitants of that capital learned on the same day, that the ships and commercial property of the Portuguese had been seized in the ports under the dominion of the Emperor Napoleon. Though this blow had been foreseen, it was not the less terrible. Some sanguine minds, however, wished to believe, that the harsh proceedings of the French government were only meant to obtain from Portugal a more effective adherence to the Continental system. The Prince Regent clung to this consolatory idea. Spain also appeared to him to afford a prop to his equivocal policy. He reckoned upon the ties of relationship, which connected him with the family of Charles IV., and still more upon the common interest which that monarch had with him, not to allow the French to obtain a footing in the peninsula ; an interest to which he had not appealed in vain during the distress of Portugal in 1797 and 1801.

But times were changed. The ruin of the house of Braganza was now plotted at Madrid as well as at Paris. Prince Masserano, a grandee of the first class, had in

France the title and honours of Spanish Ambassador. But a man without any public character had, for a year past, been the real Ambassador of Spain. Invested with the private confidence of the Prince of the Peace, Don Eugenio Izquierdo had, unknown to Masserano and the Spanish Minister for the foreign department, full powers from the King to discuss the highest concerns of the monarchy, and even to sign treaties. As he had grown old in the superintendence of the cabinet of natural history at Madrid, it was supposed that his love of science had drawn him to the metropolis of human knowledge; and this is not the first time that the cloak of the man of learning served as a cover to political intrigues. When the unseasonable rhodomontade of Godoy took place, at the time of the battle of Jena, it was Izquierdo who hurried to the Emperor's headquarters at Berlin; it was he who explained, justified, offered and promised every thing. The Prince of the Peace considered himself to have been saved by him from the wrath of Napoleon; he was at least indebted to his active agent for the powerful friend who afterwards stood him in so much stead in his day of adversity. When he despatched this secret agent to Paris, Charles *IV.* said to him, "Manuel Godoy is thy protector. Do what he orders thee. It is through him that thou must serve me." Izquierdo did so. His conduct would be irreproachable, were there not in morality a more sacred duty than that of blindly obeying the caprices of kings.

General Duroc, grand marshal of the Emperor's palace, was chosen to treat with Don Eugenio Izquierdo.

He had married a Spanish lady. No other person was entrusted with so many and such important political secrets. The turn of his mind, which had more of correctness than of profundity, his perfect steadiness, and, more than all, the empire of habit, had placed him upon the footing of a privy confidant. Another name would have been given to the connexion of Duroc with Napoleon, if a prince of his disposition could ever have a favourite.

The negotiation was carried on in secrecy. Duroc gave an account of its progress to the Emperor alone ; on his side Izquierdo corresponded with the Prince of the Peace, and with him only. The two negotiators concluded, at Fontainebleau, on the 27th of October, 1807, a treaty by which Portugal was obliterated from the list of independent states. Of the six provinces composing that kingdom, the most northern, called Entre Douro e Minho, was given in full property and sovereignty, comprehending the city of Oporto, to the King of Etruria, and was to constitute a kingdom, under the name of Northern Lusitania. The Prince of the Peace acquired the property and sovereignty of the Algarves and Alemtejo, with the title of Prince of the Algarves. The kingdom of Lusitania and the principality of the Algarves acknowledged the King of Spain as protector. The remainder of Portugal, that is to say, the provinces of Tras-os-Montes, Beira, and Estremadura, was to be sequestrated, in order, at a general peace, to be restored to the house of Braganza, in exchange for Gibraltar, the island of Trinidad, and other maritime possessions wrested from the Spaniards by the English. The Emperor of the French was to receive immediately the kingdom of Etruria ; he agreed to acknowledge the King of Spain as Emperor of the two Americas, in the same manner as he had not long before allowed the former Emperor of Germany to assume the title of Emperor of Austria.

A convention, supplementary to the treaty of Fontainebleau, and concluded on the same day, regulated the details respecting the occupation of Portugal, and the mode of its administration after the conquest. It was settled that the sequestered provinces should be governed by France. A French corps, consisting of twenty-five thousand infantry, three thousand cavalry, and an artillery establishment proportioned to this number of troops, was to receive orders to march through Spain, and, on its route, was to be supplied from the magazines of that kingdom. It was to be joined by an auxiliary Spanish corps of eight thousand foot, three thousand horse, and thirty pieces of cannon; and the conjunct force was to march direct upon Lisbon. A division of ten thousand Spaniards was to take possession of the province of Entre Douro e Minho; while another division, six thousand strong, of the same nation, was to occupy Alemtejo and the Algarves. It was agreed, that the generals in chief of the two powers should govern the country, and levy taxes for the benefit of their respective sovereigns. The Spanish generals who were placed over the northern and southern provinces of Portugal, were to be entirely independent of the general who commanded the French troops; the latter was even to obey the King of Spain or the Prince of the Peace, in case of either of them coming to the army. The sixth article of the Convention stipulated that there should be assembled, at Bayonne, an army of forty thousand men, in readiness to enter Portugal as a reinforcement; after, however, the high contracting powers should have made arrangements on this score.

On the 17th of October, 1807, Junot received orders to enter Spain within twenty-four hours. On the 18th, the van of the first division of the army of observation of the Gironde passed the Bidassoa. It was followed by the second and third divisions, the park of artillery, and the cavalry. The columns, sixteen in number, marched at a day's distance from each other, and bent their course by the high road of Burgos and Valladolid, towards Salamanca. Don Cerarco Gardoqui, intendant of the Spanish armies, had been appointed to provide for the wants of the troops. Lieutenant-general Don Pedro Rodriguez de la Buria received General Junot at Irun, and complimented him in the name of the Prince of the Peace. He had executed the same mission before, in 1801, with respect to General Leclerc.

The forces of Spain took the field at the same time, to anticipate the execution of a treaty which was not yet signed. All the regiments in the Peninsula, with the exception of the Catalonian garrisons and the troops in the camp of Saint Roch, took the road to Portugal. The corps which were habitually stationed at Madrid, and even the king's household troops, furnished detachments. In the interior of the kingdom there remained only the skeletons of battalions and squadrons, which had been stripped, to bring the field-battalions and squadrons up to their full complement; the one, of seven hundred men; the other, of a hundred and seventy horse.

The Spanish corps, which was to act under the orders of General Junot, was assembled at Alcantara, on the Tagus. Its strength was eight battalions, four squadrons, a company of horse artillery, and two companies of sappers and miners. The fine divisions of provincial grenadiers of Old and New Castile formed a part of the infantry. It was commanded by Lieutenant-general Don Juan Caraffa, Captain-general of Estremadura.

The troops which were to occupy the projected kingdom of Northern Lusitania, were drawn from Galicia, Asturias, and the kingdom of Leon, and were concentered at Tuy, on the bank of the Minho. They composed a corps of fourteen battalions, six squadrons, and a company of foot artillery, under the orders of Lieutenant-colonel Francisco Taranco y Plano, Captain-General of Galicia.

Lieutenant-general Don Francisco Solano, Marquis del Socorro, Captain-general of Andalusia, collected at Badajoz eight battalions, five squadrons, and a company of horse artillery, to take possession of the provinces which were allotted to the Prince of the Peace by the treaty of Fontainebleau.

The Spanish officers and soldiers marched with regret to an inglorious conquest. A vague uneasiness, with respect to the projects of the Emperor, began to be felt among the enlightened classes. Everywhere on its route the French army met with a favourable reception. The cities of Vittoria, Burgos, and Valladolid, gave entertainments to the General-in-chief and the principal officers. The horror which, but a few years before, the Spaniards had manifested towards a people who had been represented to them as heretics and enemies of social order, had given place to feelings of hospitable kindness. The heads of the clergy came to meet the columns. The peasants ran to the high road to see the marching by of the soldiers, who were Christians like themselves; it was obvious, that the reign of Napoleon had entirely effaced the antipathy of pre-eminently Catholic Spain to new France.

The troops were twenty-five days in reaching Salamanca. Every thing was in readiness for their being put into cantonments in the neighbourhood of that city, when Junot received orders to enter Portugal, and not to lose a moment, lest the English should anticipate him at Lisbon. The Emperor did not point out what road was to be followed, but he gave peremptory orders that *the march of the army should not be delayed for a single day, under pretence of procuring subsistence. Twenty thousand men,* said he, *con live anywhere, even in a desert.*

Of the difficulty of invading Portugal a very erroneous idea will be formed from the aspect which the configuration of that country presents on geographical maps. It would seem as if, being once established in Spain, there was only a step to make, to sever in the middle that slip of land which runs parallel with the sea, in a length of a hundred and thirty leagues, and a breadth of fifty at the utmost. The operation appears to be the more easy, from the circumstance of the Douro and the Tagus, the two great rivers of the country, flowing through Spain for the greatest part of their course; and our being taught by physical geography that, as rivers approach their mouths, the mountains dip and the valleys widen. Here it is just the contrary, and that is the reason why Portugal has remained a kingdom independent of Spain. The provinces of Entre Douro e Minho and Tras-os-Montes, to the south of the lower Douro, are more mountainous and difficult than the bordering Spanish provinces of Galicia, and especially of Leon and Zamora. Between the Douro and the Tagus, the plains of Salamanca and the valley of Plazencia terminate in Spain. The Sierra de Gata, by which they are separated, sinks in passing the Galician frontier, and then suddenly rises, at the distance of four leagues, to form the Estrella. The mass and the branches of the Estrella cover the central region of Portugal, which bears the name of Beira. The principal summit of this vast mountain is three leagues to the south-east of Guarda. It towers eight hundred fathoms above the level of the sea, and is crowned with snow throughout the year. From its granite sides flow the Zezere, the Mondego, the Alva, and thirty other tributaries of the

Tagus and the Douro. Its ramifications are sometimes formed in steep angles, sometimes in terraces of freestone blocks, heaped together in disorder. Nature and state policy have conspired together to prevent any roads of communication being made, between Portugal and Spain. across the rocks of Beira. The high road from Bayonne to Lisbon, that which is commonly used by carriages passes by Madrid, crosses the Tagus at the bridge of Almaraz in Spanish Estremadura, and a second time in front of Lisbon, where the river is three leagues wide. Military foresight did not allow the French to take a road, at the end of which, after having overcome many obstacles, they would still have to force the passage of an enormous river, or rather arm of the sea, before they could arrive at the object of their expedition. Besides, the auxiliary Spanish corps being charged to occupy the provinces on the right bank of the Douro, and the left bank of the Tagus, it appeared that the operations of the principal army ought to be central, and exclusively applied to the country comprehended between the two great rivers of Portugal.

A struggle with the difficulties of the Estrella was, therefore, inevitable. On this side there are two roads which lead to Lisbon. The one is to the north, the other to the south, of the summit of the mountain. The first goes by Almeida, Celorico, Ponte Murcella and Thomar. The narrow carts of the country, drawn by oxen, travel it with ease.

No considerable obstacles exist to the march of artillery, except the descent from the slaty table-land of

Beira-Alta into the valley of the Mondego. There are few torrents which require to be forded. On the principal river, such as the Mondago, the Alva, and the Ceira, there are bridges. The country is populous and fertile. The second road goes by Castello Branco and Abrantes. For a space of thirty leagues, it traverses a pile of rocks, a desert in which industry has contrived here and there to render productive some nooks of a wretched soil. The steep ramifications from the Sierra de Estrella run perpendicularly to the direction of the march. Every two leagues there are rivers which have neither bridges nor boats, and which in winter, or after rains, cannot be passed without extreme danger. In such excessively difficult ground, even the most feeble defence may disconcert the most experienced army. When, after having triumphed over men and nature, that army reaches Abrantes, and seems within sight of the consummation of its labours, the Tagus and the Zezere shut it out from the land of promise, and oppose an insurmountable barrier to invaders who have not been able to bring with them either artillery or a bridge equipage.

The army was in ignorance of these local details, for the geographical maps are so inaccurate, that they do not even give the names of the rivers that are to be crossed. The Portuguese themselves are better acquainted with India and Brazil than they are with the valleys of Tras-os-Montes and Beira. All the information that the French could obtain at Salamanca, was picked up from ignorant muleteers. General Junot determined to take the road to Abrantes, because it was shorter than that of Ponte Murcella. By doing this he would also gain several advantages, such as that of avoiding the fortress of Almeida, which probably would not have opened its gates, and of procuring a fresh supply of ammunition and provisions at Alcantara on the Tagus, where the Spanish division of General Caraffa was now assembling.

The army left Salamanca on the 12th of November. It marched by brigades, at intervals of a day's distance from each other : the troops had orders to go over the space of fifty leagues, between Salamanca and Alcantara, in five days. The artillery and the baggage were to accompany the columns of infantry ; the line of march that was fixed on was that by Ciudad Rodrigo, the Puerto de Perales, and Moraheja. The weather was horrible; the rain fell in torrents. Several carriages dropped behind, from the time of passing the Yeltes, before reaching Ciudad Rodrigo. In advancing, the difficulties of the march continued to increase. As neither the rapidity nor the direction of the movement had been foreseen at Madrid, provisions had not been got together, and it was impossible to collect them promptly on a frontier depopulated by former wars between Spain and Portugal. The soldiers, having nothing to eat, roamed about in the rear and on the flanks of the columns, lost themselves in the woods, and alarmed the peasants. Several perished in fording the aqueduct between Fuente Guinaldo and Pena Parda. The van of the army arrived on the Tagus in a state of wretchedness

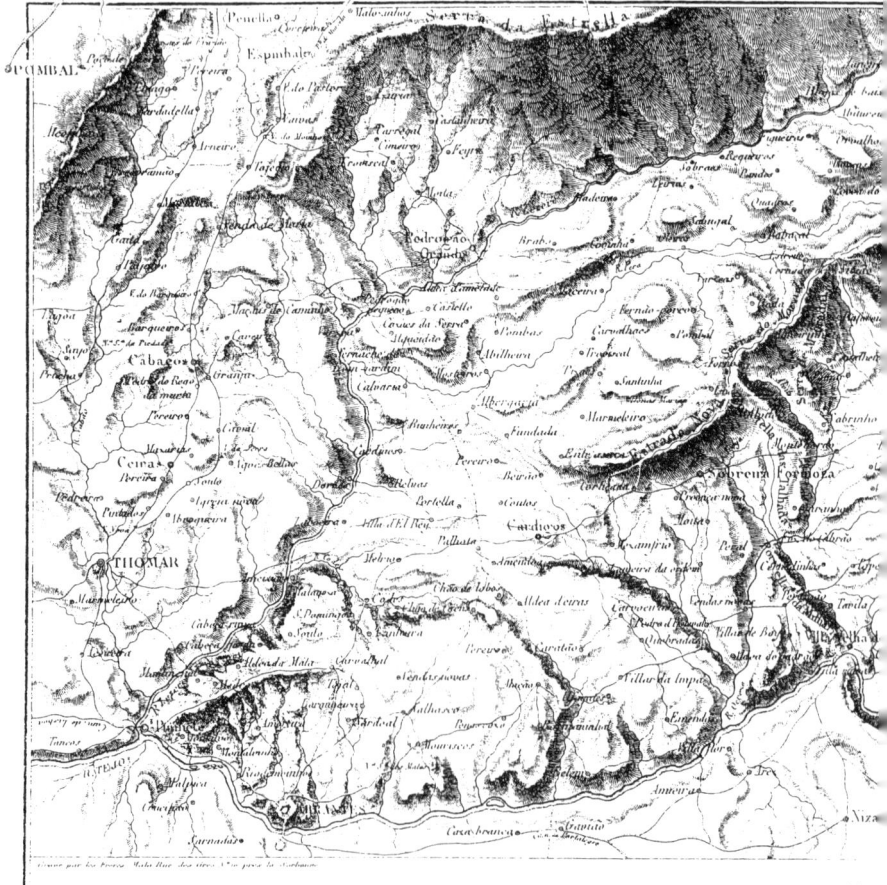

Explications

— — — Chemins suivis par l'armée Française
Anciennes fortifications de campagne
Anciens Châteaux

C
DE LA PORTI
COMPRISE ENTRE L
Pour serv
DE LA CAM
Dressée par le Chef de Bat.on J. M. C
POUR SON HISTOIRE D

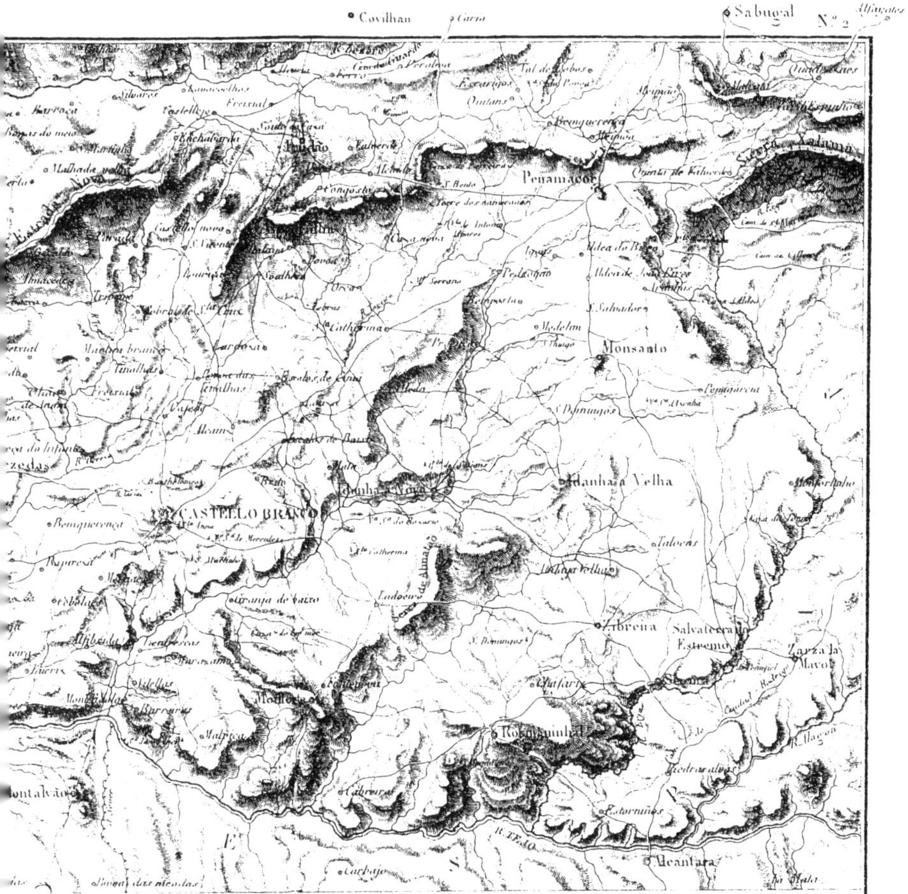

TE
DU PORTUGAL
EZERE ET LE TAGE,
ntelligence
E DE 1807
sous les yeux du Général FOY
ERRE DE LA PENINSULE.

Echelles de 2mill ½ pour 1000 Mètres

Lieues de Portugal de 18 au Degré

Lieues d'Espagne de 17 ½ au Degré

Lieues d'Espagne de 26 au Degré

Kilomètres et Myriamètres

Lieues Communes de France de 25 au Degré

Milles Anglais de 69 ½ au Degré

au Méridien de Paris

and confusion, which was the forerunner of still greater wretchedness and confusion.

General Junot reached Alcantara two days before the troops. This city, situated on the left bank of the Tagus, is famous for its bridge, a magnificent work of the Romans. it was formerly looked upon as one of the principal Spanish frontier fortresses against Portugal, though its fortifications consist of nothing more than a miserable envelope, with saliant and re-entering angles, without a covered way, and without a moat. No military establishments were found there. General Caraffa had been a week in the city. The depopulation of the country had not admitted of replacing in the magazines and in the depôts of cattle, the bread and meat which his division had consumed. Hardly one or two rations per man could be given to the French. Their damaged cartridges were exchanged for fresh ammunition. By coming to Alcantara the troops had lengthened their march four leagues. The general-in-chief, therefore, ordered that those who had not arrived, and the whole of the carriages, should not advance farther on this route than Zarza-la-Major. In spite of famine, the rain, ignorance as to the roads, and the uncertainty what enemies there would be to encounter, he did not hesitate as to the steps to be taken. In his situation, to march was to fight, and to arrive would he to conquer. By the order of the day of the 17th of November, the corps of observation of the Gironde was informed, that it would enter Portugal before the expiration of forty-eight hours. A proclamation, issued on the same day from the headquarters at Alcantara, informed the Portuguese that the armies of Napoleon were entering their country, in order to make common cause with their beloved sovereign against the tyrant of the seas. As usual, the inhabitants were invited to remain quiet in their towns and villages, and were threatened with the customary penalties, in case of their taking arms against their allies the French. As a great number of soldiers, a part of the artillery, and all the bag-gage, had fallen behind, Adjutant-commandant Bagneris received orders to wait at Zarza-la-Major for the detachments, stragglers, and carriages, which successively arrived, and to form the whole into a column, with which he was to follow the last division of the army.

On the 19th of November, a company of light troops took post at Segura, a Portuguese village, of whose ancient castle, demolished in former wars, only a half-ruined tower is now standing. On the same day, the vanguard, consisting of the seventieth regiment of infantry, two companies of Catalonian sappers and miners, and the Spanish hussar regiment of Maria Louisa, under the orders of Brigadier-general Maurin, began the march of the army. It was followed, next day, by the first and second divisions of infantry, and by that of General Caraffa. These forces entered Portugal by the bridge of Segura, on the Erjas, and called in the company of light troops which had been pushed forward. The rest of the army set out, on the succeeding days, and forded the Erjas, at the foot of the mountain on which are the remains of the dismantled fortress of Salvaterra do Estremo.

The march was directed on Castello Branco. The advanced guard took the best but longest road, which goes through the small town of Idanha a Nova. The other part of the army proceeded in two columns; the one by Zibreira and Ledoviro; the other, by Rosmarinhal and Monforte. Both of them forded the Aravil and the Poncul, rivers which fall into the Tagus.

Castello Branco is built on the slope of a hill, and is over-looked by an old castle. In 1704 Marshal Berwick ordered a part of its walls to be blown up. The Spanish army, under Count d'Aranda, and the auxiliary corps, commanded by the Prince of Beauvau, were not able to penetrate farther than this town in 1762. It is a bishopric, and the principal town of a comarca. It has a population of six thousand inhabitants, which in such a country is a considerable number.

The troops spent but one night at Castello Branco, and continued their progress in two columns. The advanced guard and the second division proceeded by Perdigao and Macao; the road is practicable for man and horse, and there are but few torrents. At the Portella da Milharica this road crosses the steep mountains which run perpendicularly to the Tagus, from the summit of the Moradal to behind VillaVelha, and which, after having contracted the stream between two rocks, stretch out towards Niza, in the Alemtejo. This difficult chain is traversed, or rather rent open, by the river Ocreza, which is not fordable anywhere near its confluence with the Tagus. The troops passed it in front of Vendas Novas by a ferry-boat, which could not contain more than twelve men, or four horses. It was with extreme slowness, and not without the loss of some soldiers, that eight or ten thousand men, and eight or nine hundred horses, were conveyed from the one bank to the other.

The general staff, the first division, the greatest part of the columns of the rear-guard, and whatever artillery-waggons they could carry with them, took the upper road, which is wider than the other, but thickly set with blocks of quartz and rocky asperities. At every step swollen and rapid rivers tried the patience of the troops, and swept some of them away. Besides several torrents of less magnitude, they were obliged successively to ford the Liria, the Ocreza, which was then four feet in depth; the Alvito, still wider, and nearly as deep; and the Troya the passage of which would have been looked upon as very dangerous, if the Alvito and the Ocreza had not previously been crossed. On the right bank of the Alvito rises perpendicularly the chain which comes from Moradal. The pass which leads through this chain is called Portella das Thalhadas. On the right and left of the road, the army saw the remains of the redoubts which were constructed by the Count de Lippe, when, in the campaign of 1762, he wished to add to the strength of this strong position. After a fifteen hours' march the stoutest and nimblest of the men reached Sobreira Formoza. The French stopped but a night in that village. Other torrents, other mountains awaited them, almost all the way to Abrantes. Old soldiers, who had served in the Swiss and Tyrolese Alps, were astonished when they found it necessary to descend almost vertically into the bed of the Codes, and then scale the wall of rocks on the left bank of that tributary stream of the Zezere. During five deadly days, cheerless eminences of freestone succeed wastes of sharp slaty rocks, and are followed by enormous mountains of granite. Here, wherever the stone does not appear on the surface, the eye wanders till it is lost over wastes uniformly strewed with heath and cistus. The only flocks of the inhabitants are lean goats, so timid that they are always ready to fly to the mountains. To find the traces of human beings, they must he sought for at the bottom of some ravines, which retain water in summer. There, near a hamlet, which, in the colour and the shape of its houses, resembles a continuation of the eternal rock, some enclosures are planted with olives, and a little rye and maize is sown. The monotony of the landscape is relieved by nothing but insulated chestnut-trees, which were then leafless, the pale cork-trees, and the stunted green oaks, the appearance of which has, at all seasons, a melancholy effect.

The army suffered incessantly from the bad weather. In Portugal, the autumnal rains are a positive deluge, which reminds us of the winter of the Antilles. Twenty times a day the columns of infantry were broken in fording the swollen and overflown rivers. The soldiers straggled along at random; and, ceasing to be restrained by the ties of discipline and the presence of their leaders, they had no longer the appearance of an army, but rather of a medley of individuals exasperated by distress. The day's march was a very long one. The narrow paths often obliged them to proceed one by one. In a country where the mountains are so lofty, the sun is scarcely eight hours above the horizon. It was not till a late hour of the night that they could reach their resting-place. And what a resting-place! almost always the naked rock. In the German wars, a smoking stove and kind hosts made the French forget the toils of a forced march. In Portugal, it was a God-send when, after having endured the most terrible fatigues they could obtain the shelter of a green oak; when, from the scrubby olive trees, they could procure fuel enough to make a fire, which, after all, had not heat enough to dry their body and their clothes, drenched as they were by the rains of heaven and the streams.

The French were not expected in Portugal; no preparation had been made to receive them, either as friends or as enemies. It was known in Beira that they were coasting along the frontier. As the magistrates received from Lisbon neither orders nor advice, as to the conduct that was to be observed towards them, it was supposed that the French army would pass the Tagus, in the Spanish territory, to proceed to Gibraltar. This opinion gained ground when it was discovered that the first columns had taken the direction of Alcantara. Yet, all at once, behold them entering Portugal, with no provisions, no means of transport, and pushing on without stop through a country in which a prudent traveller never quits the place where he has slept without providing subsistence for the day.

Accordingly, no distribution of provisions was made. Castello Branco, the only place on the road which could have furnished bread, meat, and wine, was taken at unawares, and was, in a manner, stunned by the irruption of the foreign troops. Notwithstanding several examples of severity, which the commander-in-chief exercised on offending French and Spaniards, less as a punishment for unavoidable faults, than to prevent the recurrence of disorder at a time when it would not be so excusable, the plundering which took place hindered the inhabitants from applying to the use of the army the scanty resources which they might have been able to collect together under ordinary circumstances. Pressed by want, the soldiers betook themselves to the commons, and ate the honey from the hives which are scattered about in those situations. Some discovered and devoured the frugal hoard of maize, olives, and chestnuts, which the poor peasant had put by to feed his family during the winter; others lived on the acorns, *bellotas,* with which cattle are fattened in the Peninsula. Woe to the humble cottage that fell in the way of these famished marauders! The terrified families immediately took flight. Many soldiers of the infantry were killed by the peasants, who were driven to despair. The cavalry lost a still greater number of horses; even the strongest were unshod, meagre, and worn out. From the first day after the passing of the Erjas, the artillery fell into the rear, though twelve oxen or horses were harnessed to each field-piece, and though, in scaling the mountains, they were rather carried than drawn up by the artillerymen and the soldiers assigned for the service of the park.

General Junot arrived at Abrantes on the morning of the 24th. His advanced guard had entered that town the evening before. His first care was to secure the passage of the Zezere. The occupation of Abrantes was to be completed, in a military point of view, by taking possession of Punhete, a small town, situated on the left bank of the Zezere, at its confluence with the Tagus. Mezeur, captain of engineers, the Catalan sappers and miners, and a detachment of French infantry, were accordingly dispatched to Punhete to re-establish a bridge, formed of boats, which, after having been used for that purpose in 1801, were now scattered about in various parts of the river. Abrantes is a considerable city. It is built on the southern slope of an eminence, at the foot of which flows the Tagus. The entrance to it is by narrow and difficult roads; the upper part has old walls and a ruined castle. There is a permanent bridge of boats a quarter of a league below the walls of the city. It is the last on the road to Lisbon. Not far from here, the Tagus, enlarged by the Zezere, ceases to flow in an abyss, and descends to the sea, majestic, immense, and watering the fertile plains which are situated at the termination of the desert, and at the entrance of Alemtejo, on one side, and of Estremadura on the other. The fortress of Abrantes might be made to have a great influence upon military operations. It only wants to be better fortified to be the key of Portugal.

At Abrantes the sufferings of the army terminated. Provisions and shoes were given out to the soldiers. The doubts which had hitherto been felt as to the steps which the Court of Lisbon would take, and the just fears of the English effecting a landing at the mouth of the Tagus, now vanished before consolatory hopes. If the Prince Regent had intended to resort to force of arms to prevent foreigners entering his kingdom, there was nothing to hinder him from opposing the French with more than ten thousand troops, collected beforehand in the vicinity of his capital. The regulars and the militia would have garrisoned Abrantes, or, at least they would have occupied the entrenchments which still existed on the right bank of the Zezere, opposite Punhete. On the contrary, the moral aspect of the country was quiet and peaceable. The success of the expedition was no longer problematical. With a sort of openness of heart, which, however, was not wholly without calculation, the French General himself announced to the Portuguese Prime Minister his arrival at Abrantes. " I shall be at Lisbon in our days," said he. " My soldiers are quite disconsolate that they have not yet fired a shot. Do not compel them to do it. I think you will be in the wrong if you do."

Portugal was conquered, and the Prince Regent did not even know that foreign troops had set foot in his kingdom. After the departure of the French legation and the Spanish embassy from Lisbon, the government had advised the merchants of the English factory not to wait the issue of a quarrel which, whatever might be its result, could not fail to terminate to their prejudice; to hasten their removal, it relinquished the custom-house duties payable upon exported merchandise. Three hundred English families, almost denationalised by their long residence in those cities, immediately left Lisbon and Oporto with their property. A promise was given to respect the persons and property of those who stayed. On this condition, and with the understanding that the French and Spaniards should not enter Portugal, England allowed the Court of Lisbon to yield an ostensible obedience to the will of the Emperor Napoleon.

Encouraged by this permission, the government wrote to Paris, that it would take part, fully and absolutely, in the continental system, and was preparing to declare war against England; but it pleaded that the particular situation of the country and its maritime and commercial interests, rendered xtreme prudence necessary. Richly laden vessels were expected from America. A Portuguese squadron was then cruising before Algiers, and would infallibly fail into the hands of the English, if hostilities were commenced before it had time to return to the Tagus. Brazil was destitute of fortifications and troops. It was of importance to the powers that had united against the supremacy of a single state, that it should not add this rich portion of the American Continent to its already too numerous possessions. To prevent Brazil from becoming an

JUNOT'S INVASION

English colony, the Prince Regent offered to send his eldest son with the title of Constable, to revive in his subjects of the New World their affection for the mother country. The Prince of Beira was then only nine years old, but the Princess Dowager of Brazil, the Queen's sister, who was beloved by the people, and was considered as the strongest minded individual of the house of Braganza, should accompany the Prince and govern in his name, with the assistance of the late Viceroy, Don Fernando de Portugal. It was hoped at Lisbon that this resolution, which was notified at the same time to the nation and to foreign courts, would be in unison with the political views of France. If, however, the hope of the Prince should be disappointed, he must, as he had often declared, adopt, though with reluctance, the measure of withdrawing with his family from n his European dominions.

Notwithstanding this, the intelligence received from Paris did not cease to be alarming. The Portuguese Ambassador had only vague suspicions with respect to the machinations and intrigues which preceded the treaty of Fontainebleau; but he saw the troops assembling at Bayonne. His letters, which grew every day more pressing, at last decided the Cabinet of Lisbon to issue an official declaration of war against England. By his edict of the 20th of October, the Prince Regent announced that, finding it impossible to preserve any longer a neutrality which was so advantageous to his subjects, he had determined to join the cause of the Continent, and to shut his ports against British vessels, commercial as well as warlike. On the twenty second of October, the Portuguese Ambassador in England signed, in the name of the same Prince, an eventual Convention, by which the Court of London agreed to tolerate the closing of the Lusitanian ports, provided France did not require any thing further; and engaged to furnish active assistance to convey the Court of Lisbon to Brazil, in case the extravagant demands of the common enemy should render that measure necessary.

The more hesitation and difficulty there was in the line of conduct pursued by the Portuguese government, the more it strove to induce a belief that it had entered sincerely into the new system of political ideas. A levy of recruits was ordered, to raise to twelve hundred men the regiments of infantry, which were all incomplete. On the same day, the Prince Regent decreed the putting on foot of two militia regiments of Eastern and Western Lisbon, and the erection of a new corps of cavalry, under the name of the Royal Horse Volunteers. Officers of the engineers and artillery were sent to the Peninsula of Peniche, and the maritime forts, to repair and arm them, and increase their means of attack and defence. Batteries, intended to produce a cross fire with those on the right bank, were marked out on the left bank of the Tagus. Moveable batteries were organised on the coast. Several corps, which, like the rest of the army, had never before stirred from their usual garrisons, were now removed. A brigade, composed of two regiments stationed in the capital, the fourth and the tenth of infantry, were cantoned at Carcabelos, near the mouth of the Tagus, with orders to oppose any landing which the enemy might attempt, and, in case of need, to throw themselves into the forts. The thirteenth regiment of infantry also quitted Lisbon to garrison Peniche, which had hitherto been guarded only by invalide soldiers. The light legion rein forced the garrison of Setubal. Camps were projected at Barcellos, to the north of the Douro; at Soura, near Coimbre; at Mafra; and at Alcacer do Sal, to the south of the Tagus. In the mean while, till these could be formed, there appeared to be established a sufficient lime of observation to watch over the safety of the coast.

Still more animation was manifested in the naval service. Squadrons were required to defend the entrance of the Tagus against the English fleet. Viscount Anadia, the secretary of state for this department, was seen to tear himself all at once from his mild and indolent habits, hurry to the arsenal at day-break, and spend his time wholly on board the ships. Every vessel in the navy, that was thought sea-worthy, was refitted, equipped, and provisioned, without a moment's delay.

The royal treasury was exhausted; money became daily more scarce. Yet an increase in the receipts was necessary, to cover the expenses incurred by augmenting and putting in motion the land and sea forces. Individuals were invited, by a royal decree, to bring their plate to the mint, either as a gift or a loan, or to be coined on their own account. The Prince Regent set the example, and converted a part of the crown plate into new cruzadoes.

OF PORTUGAL

JUNOT'S INVASION

Even those persons, however, who were the least clear-sighted, remarked, that there was more of show than reality in all this parade of defensive preparations; and that those means of which the efficacy was most obvious, might be applied to uses quite different from that which was avowed. Thus, the fleet being provisioned for several months, there 'vas nothing to prevent it from being employed in conveying to Brazil the royal family and the grandees of the kingdom. The plate, by being converted into coin, could be removed with more ease. The regiments collected in the vicinity of Lisbon might serve to protect the departure of the Prince against a popular insurrection, which was naturally to be expected; and, in case of being pressed by foreign troops, the forts, made tenable and furnished with artillery, and especially the fort of Peniche, might, by their resistance, gain the time which was requisite for effecting the embarkation regularly and without disorder.

It was not without reason that the Court of Lisbon was suspicious of its new allies. The storm which was brewing against it was gathering with frightful rapidity. The Ambassadors of Portugal were dismissed from Paris and Madrid. By his presence at Lisbon, Don Lorenço de Lima gave additional weight to the arguments with which he had filled his correspondence. He had seen the corps of observation of the Gironde in full march through Spain. Regret was now felt that recourse had been had to temporising. Notwithstanding the promises made to England, the Prince Regent, on the 8th of November, signed an order to place guards over the few British subjects who had remained at Lisbon, and to sequestrate their property. He quieted his scrupulous conscience by reflecting on the facilities and delays which he had granted, in order to enable them to place their persons and properties in security.

There was no time to be lost. Above all things it was necessary to stop the march of the French army, and appease Napoleon. Don Pedro-Jose-Joaquim Vito de Menezes, Marquis of Marialva, one of the nobles of the court, who was most qualified by birth, and most distinguished for the cultivation of his mind, was dispatched to the Emperor. He was instructed to offer pecuniary sacrifices, and, as a mark of personal respect to the Emperor, he was to propose a marriage between the Prince of Beira, the future heir to the throne, and one of the daughters of the Grand-duke of Berg.

The events of the war prevented M. de Marialva from going further than Madrid. But had he reached Paris, his mission would have had no better success. It was not merely to occupy two great ports on the ocean that the Emperor had sent his troops beyond the Pyrenees. The whole of the Peninsula was included within the scope of his gigantic projects. The secret collusion between Portugal and England had not eluded his vigilance, and it ministered to his policy in the system which was then protected by victory: since the house of Braganza chose to betray the cause of the Continent, it must cease to reign.

JUNOT'S INVASION

In the day when her ally of a century old was in distress, England did not attempt to commit her armies in an unequal contest with the combined forces of France and Spain. But, though unable to defend the Portuguese, she wished at least to share in their spoils. Sir Sidney Smith, famous for having at St. John of Acre, given a slight check to the fortunate career of Napoleon, sailed from England, early in November, with a squadron, to escort the Prince Regent to Brazil, or, in case of his refusal, to take possession of his fleet. As there might be some obstacles in the way of this operation, instructions were sent to Lieutenant-general Sir John Moore, who was then proceeding with seven thousand men from Sicily to the Baltic, to call at Lisbon, and concur in carrying the plan into effect. Another corps of troops, which was assembled at Portsmouth, under the orders of Major-general Sir Brent Spencer, was to be forwarded to the same country, should there appear to be a likelihood of meeting with any resistance. General Beresford was dispatched with a regiment to occupy the island of Madeira. Orders were sent to the East Indies, to seize Goa and the other Portuguese establishments. English foresight did not forget even the factory of Macao in China.

Lord Strangford, a man less known at the time by his diplomatic services than by his success in elegant literature, was the minister plenipotentiary from his Britannic Majesty to the Prince Regent. Notwithstanding the official declaration of the 20th of October, he had continued to reside at Lisbon, and to negotiate with the ministers. He announced to them that, "in consenting to overlook the insult of exclusion from the Portuguese ports, the King of England granted every thing that the difficulty of circumstances and the recollection of an ancient alliance could justly require; but that a single instance more of subserviency to France would inevitably draw down reprisals." The effect followed close upon the threat. As soon as Viscount Strangford was informed of the order issued for detaining his countrymen, he took down the arms of England from over the gate of his hotel, and demanded his passports. A few days after he removed on board the Hibernia, the Admiral's ship of the English fleet, which had arrived off the bar of Lisbon. In obedience to his instructions from the ministry, Rear-admiral Sir Sidney Smith declared the Tagus and the Portuguese coast in a state of blockade.

From the windows of his palace of Mafra, the Prince Regent saw the vessels of Great Britain giving chase to the ships of his subjects. By land as by sea, every thing around him was hostile. In consequence of having endeavoured to keep well with two rival powers, he was on the point of losing all, without even the consolation of having saved his honour. Woeful condition for a sovereign, whose courtiers could not believe in the patriotism and devotedness of the nation, because there was nothing in their own hearts but selfishness and pusillamimity!

The merchant ships of Lisbon and Oporto were seized and taken into the English ports on the very day on which the French, passing the Erjas, began to pillage the cottages of the peasants of Beira. The want of posts and roads, and the negligence of the Administration, caused their march to remain unknown. They were supposed to have stopped at Salamanca, or, at the utmost, advanced only as far as Alcantara, when, on the evening of the 24th of November, the government received the letter, dated at Abrantes, from their general-in-chief. By a singular coincidence it happened that, on the same day, the 24th of November, there arrived at the English fleet a messenger from London, who brought the number of the Moniteur, in which it was stated that the house of Braganza had ceased to reign, and brought also an assurance that, forgetting the past, England was ready to restore its friendship to the Prince Regent, if he would consent to depart to Brazil, but that it would never suffer the Portuguese navy to fall into the hands of France.

The surest way of preventing this, would have been to seize it. But this could not be accomplished without taking the forts on the Tagus, and the troops under Generals Moore and Spencer were not yet arrived. Sir Sidney Smith sent a message on shore, and backed it by pressing letters. Lord Strangford landed: an extraordinary council of state was convoked, and the situation of the house of Braganza and of the monarchy was discussed in the presence of the Prince. England guaranteed the colonial possessions.

From France, on the contrary, there was nothing to be expected but the execution of the sentence pronounced by the terrible Moniteur. After all, it was better to reign in America than to be a prisoner in Europe. To make such an evident fact as this clear to the dullest understanding, did not require the vehemence of Sir Sidney Smith, or the rhetoric of Lord Strangford. It was a more eloquent counsellor than the two Englishmen, it was fear, that at last overcame the perpetual fluctuation of the Prince Regent: he resolved to embark.

On the breaking up of the council, the royal family went to the castle of Queluz, two leagues from Lisbon, in order to he nearer to the quay of Belem, where the preparations to embark were to be made. The result of the deliberation was communicated to the principal persons of the government and the court, and to those whom the Prince Regent himself selected to accompany him to Brazil. The marine brigade went on board the ships. The captains of the royal and commercial vessels were authorised to receive, in those births which were not appropriated by authority, all such faithful subjects as were willing to run the risk of emigrating, and, among these, the preference was to be given to naval and military officers. The custom-house was ordered not to claim the export duties on the luggage and goods of the emigrants. The major part of the persons employed in the government offices requested to be allowed to follow the fortunes of the Prince, and many were refused. There was not room enough in the vessels for all those whom the fear of foreign troops induced to share the fate of their sovereign The moveables of the court and of individuals were shipped in the utmost disorder. For three days, Belem quay was blocked up with carriages, precious effects, and heavy bales and chests, which were in a manner abandoned to the mercy of the first comer.

The twenty-fifth of November was spent by the government in devising means to diminish the confusion and collision which could not fail to arise from the unforeseen march of foreign armies. An order was sent to the civil magistrates, and to the governors of fortresses and provinces, to receive the French and Spanish troops. In the mean while, the Chevalier d'Araujo despatched a Portuguese merchant, José Oliviera de Barreto, a part of whose family was settled in France, to meet General Junot, for the purpose of parleying with him and gaining time.

On the twenty-sixth, a decree, which was published and posted in the streets of Lisbon, announced to the Portuguese people that the Prince had resolved to remove to the American provinces, with the queen, his family, and the court, and to fix his residence at Rio de Janeiro, till the conclusion of a general peace. "Notwithstanding he had exhausted the public treasury, and had made continually repeated sacrifices, he had not," he said, " been able to succeed in preserving the blessings of peace to his beloved subjects. The French troops were on their march towards the capital: to resist would be to shed the blood of brave men, without any benefit to their native land. Being himself more particularly the object of the unprovoked hatred of the Emperor Napoleon, he departed with those belonging to him, that he might lighten the burthen of calamity which pressed on the country."

On the morning of the 27th, the streets and squares were thronged with weeping citizens. The royal family set out from Queluz sooner than had been expected, to proceed to the place of embarkation. Guards had been forgotten to be stationed on the shore at Belem. The multitude crowded round the carriages. The coach of the old Queen was at the head of the mournful procession. Sixteen years had passed by, since she had been seen by the people. Doomed during that long period to outlive herself, she had recently recovered, together with a gleam of reason sufficient to show her the calamities of her country, the noble feelings of a Portuguese and a Queen. She was repeatedly heard to exclaim, "What! shall we quit the kingdom without having fought!" When her coachman strove to quicken the pace of his horses, that he might get rid of the pressure of the crowd, "Not so fast," said she; "it will be thought we are running away." The Princess of Brazil met the blows of misfortune with equal firmness. Her numerous children, so lately the hope of the nation, burst into tears by the side of their mother. The Prince Regent came last. When he stepped from the carriage, he could hardly walk; his limbs trembled under him. With his hand he put aside the people who clung round his knees. Tears trickled from his eyes, and his countenance told plainly enough how woe-begone and perplexed was his heart. In abandoning the spot where the ashes of his forefathers reposed, his disturbed imagination depicted to him a futurity as gloomy and terrible as the tempest which rends the ocean, to which he was now for the first time going to commit himself.

When the wind is in some points of the compass, ships cannot get out of the Tagus. For forty hours contrary weather prevented the fleet from sailing. These forty hours were an age to the embarked court. The French, who seemed to have fallen from the clouds into Abrantes, might, without any miracle, have quitted that city after having rested two days, and might appear all at once in the middle of Lisbon. Apprehensive of the consequences of a prolonged delay, the Prince Regent ordered the artillery to be removed from some of the forts which could cannonade the fleet, and the guns of the batteries were begun to be spiked.

During the whole of the 28th, groups of citizens, and of the peasants of the environs, thronged the summits of the hills which are near the mouth of the Tagus. Every eye was fixed upon the squadron. But the public grief had now assumed another character. That which had rendered it so expansive on the preceding evening was, that the minds of the multitude had been disposed to melancholy by the terrific perspective of the future. Each, while he shed tears for the royal family, had first wept his own fate. Other reflections now took their place : the Prince no longer made common cause with his people; the nation was conquered without having been vanquished. Priests, nobles, soldiers, plebeians, all turned their thoughts sadly inwards; all began to think of their own safety. Many fled from the capital, which was soon to be polluted by the presence of foreign troops.

On the morning of the 29th, a favourable wind sprang up from the land. The Portuguese fleet weighed anchor. It consisted of eight sail of the line, three frigates, three brigs, and a considerable number of merchantmen. On leaving the bar, it passed through the English squadron, which was under sail, and which received it with the customary honours. At the moment when the twenty-one guns of the royal salute were heard at Lisbon, there was an eclipse of the sun. Some superstitious Portuguese then exclaimed, in the words of the Parisian Moniteur, "The House of Braganza has ceased to reign!"

While the royal family remained in sight, Lisbon seemed to be sunk in a deadly stupor. As soon as it was gone, fear and despair produced confusion. The whole thirteenth regiment of infantry hurried to Peniche, without orders, on hearing of the Prince's embarkation. The city was full of soldiers who quitted their colours in parties. The English were still seen off the bar; for when he departed with four sail to convoy the Portuguese fleet to Brazil, Rear-admiral Sir Sidney Smith left the remainder of his squadron to continue the blockade of the Tagus.

The French were not far distant, for their General had not been idle at Abrantes. While the extraordinary rise of the waters and the violence of the current retarded the establishment of the bridge at Punhete, he assembled the first troops of his army, and gave a new organisation to his advanced guard. The grenadier and light companies of the first and second divisions were united in battalions. General Caraffa, with a part of his Spanish corps, occupied Thomar, to collect provisions. Large boats were got ready on the Tagus, to convey to Lisbon the sick and the cannon, on their arrival at Abrantes. Three hundred infantry, to escort this convoy, were embarked in smaller boats, from which they could easily land on either bank. It was resolved, that the artillery horses should march separately from the carriages, and should follow by land the movement of that part which went by water. To the reserves of artillery and the column of equipages, which had halted at Zarza la Mayor, instructions were sent to enter Portugal by the route of Alcantara and Badajoz. As soon as the General had got together eight or ten thousand men, he did not wait for the rest : orders were issued for the troops to begin their march towards Lisbon.

On the 26th, the advanced guard, consisting of four picked battalions, commanded by Colonel Grandsaigne, the principal aid-de-camp of the general-in-chief, and also of the regiment of Spanish hussars, proceeded to Punhete. On the following day, it passed the Zezere in boats. The other troops followed at a distance. The bridge could not be completed before one half of the army had reached the opposite bank. Junot was at the head of his van-guard; on the other side of the river he found José Oliveira de Barreto, who had arrived from Lisbon. The Commander d'Araujo intreated the General-in-chief to suspend the progress of the army, and to send forward a confidential person, with whom the details respecting the occupation of the territory might be settled advantageously for both nations. From this envoy the French general learned the resolution of the Prince Regent to transfer his government and court to America.

Junot in his heart rejoiced at the Prince Regent's determination. The presence of the sovereign, whom he must either have treated with respect, or oppressed, could have tended only to embarrass the establishment of the French in Portugal. He, however, continued his march, not in the hope of arriving time enough to seize the fleet in the Tagus, but because it was impossible, without the means of subsistence, to stop an army which was irritated by long privations. Herman, the late French consul in Portugal, was despatched from the headquarters at Punhete, to concert measures with the Commander d'Araujo. When he entered Lisbon, the Regent and his ministers, who had been six-and-thirty hours on board, were anxiously waiting for a wind to carry them out to sea.

The distance between Abrantes and Lisbon is five-and-twenty leagues. The road is a good one for carriages. It passes through the fertile fields on the right bank of the Tagus. The continuance of the autumnal rains had made the river and its tributary streams overflow. The advanced guard and a part of the first division, crossed the plain of Golegao with the water up to their knees. The other troops took a circuitous route by Torres Novas and Pernes. They thus avoided the inundations of the Alviela and the Almonda, as they passed those rivers at points more distant from their confluence with the Tagus. The inhabitants of the country did not quit their houses on the approach of the French. Provisions were found at Santarem, a city which contains a population of ten thousand, and is one of the finest and best situated in the kingdom. The stragglers, who, in consequence of the bad weather and the difficulty of the road, were still numerous, carried terror into the insulated farm-houses, and into those charming *quintas,* which are the ornament of the Portuguese valleys; so rooted in the troops had become the habit of pillage which they had acquired during their sufferings in Beira!

The van of the army reached Sacavem at ten o'clock on the evening of the 29th. Sacavem, which is a village two leagues from Lisbon, is joined to that capital. by an uninterrupted series of country houses. It was a post which it was important to occupy, in consequence of its defence being rendered easy by a lengthened bay, which is there crossed on a flying bridge. On the road, the French general met Lieutenant-general Martinho de Souza e Abuquerque and Brigadier Francisco de Borja Garçao Stockler, who were sent by the Council of Government to compliment him. Next arrived deputations from the city and the commercial part of its inhabitants, which had been spontaneously formed from among persons of the middle class, to whom either their situation or their opinions gave an interest in winning the good-will of the new government. They both announced the departure of the royal family. They also described the agitated state of the people, and asserted that the English fleet had land forces on board, and that it seemed to be manoeuvring to force the passage of the bar. The General-in-chief desired the general officers to return to Lisbon, and to notify to the governors of the kingdom, that he should hold them responsible for the preservation of the public peace. To the other deputies he recommended, to calm the minds of their fellow-citizens, and to tell them that, for the second time, Portugal was about to be indebted to France for her independence. A proclamation, speaking the same sentiments as he now verbally expressed, was given to them, to be immediately translated into Portuguese, printed in the two languages, and profusely distributed and posted.

Yet, even while thus affecting calmness and confidence, Junot was overwhelmed with anxious cares; he was perfectly aware, that, in the present situation of his army, there was no medium for it between success and utter ruin. The rain was still falling in torrents; the west wind, which had blown continually for a month, might bring the English fleet in an hour's time before the quays of Lisbon. Ten thousand soldiers, and thirty thousand inhabitants capable of bearing arms, were brought in contact with each other, and mutually communicated their grief and their enthusiastic feelings. The columns of the French army, meanwhile, marched slowly, and almost at random, separated from each other by torrents and inundated plains. The nearest of them had halted at Santarem, because General Delaborde, who was at its head, wished to get together at least a third of his troops. The succeeding division was two marches behind. There was no news of General Travot, or his cavalry, or of the artillery. It was not known whether the Spanish armies, which were to invade Alemtejo and Entre Douro e Minho, had even begun to move. If the General-in-chief had fifteen hundred men with him at Sacavem, that was the utmost; and they were in bad order and worn out with fatigue.

At particular moments men are acted upon, are smitten with astonishment, are subjugated, much oftener by moral force, which is in its nature indefinite, than by physical force, the probable effects of which are within the scope of calculation. Junot resolved not to allow the Portuguese time to learn from hostile reports the disorder of his march, and the scanty number of his soldiers. He entered the capital of Portugal at the head of the skeletons or rather the wrecks of his four picked battalions, on the 30th of November, 1807, a hundred and sixty-seven years, exactly to a day, since the overthrow of the Spanish tyranny by the Portuguese. The French general hastened to Belem, ordered the Prince Regent's cannoneers to fire on some vessels of the royal fleet, which had remained behind, and were endeavouring to join the convoy, compelled them to put back into the port, garrisoned with his infantry the closed batteries on both sides of the Tagus, and returned to the city with the officers of his staff, having no other escort than thirty Portuguese horsemen.

The signs prelusive of a tempest vanished suddenly. The public tranquillity was not disturbed. The usual labours of the day were not suspended. Pickets of the Portuguese royal police-guard served as guides to the French troops, and conducted them to their allotted barracks. They had at last made their entrance, those formidable warriors before whom Europe was dumb and whose looks the Prince Regent had not dared to encounter. A people possessed of a lively imagination had expected to see heroes of a superior species, colossuses, demigods. The French were nothing but men. A forced march of eighteen days, famine, torrents, inundated valleys, and beating rain, had debilitated their bodies, and destroyed their clothing. They had hardly strength enough left to keep the step to the sound of the drum. A long file of lean, limping, and mostly beardless soldiers, followed with lagging pace the scantily filled masses of the battalions. The officers, the generals themselves, were worn out, and it may be said disfigured, by long and excessive fatigue. The artillery, which is called *ultima ratio regum*, did not even march with the column of infantry. For the purposes of attack and defence, the troops had nothing but rusted firelocks, and cartridges imbued with water. The Portuguese had been prepared to feel terror; the only feeling which they now experienced was that of vexation, at having been astounded and brought under the yoke by a handful of foreigners. This contemptuous estimate of the French forces, in which every one indulged in proportion to the fear that he had felt, left in the minds of the people the seeds of revolt which were soon ripened into vigorous existance by the course of events.

BOOK II.

ON the morrow after the entrance of the French, there was at Lisbon a slight shock of an earthquake, which made the sea flow upon the quays. It was at this moment that the General-in-chief was giving an account of his expedition to Clarke, the minister at war. "The gods are favourable to us," wrote he; "I draw the omen of it from the circumstance of the earthquake having only manifested their power, without doing us any injury."

It was the joy inspired by success that prompted these words, and Junot felt that joy the more strongly, from his having been so near failing in his enterprise. The army joined its General gradually and by scraps. The stragglers had quartered themselves, twenty or thirty together, in the lone houses, and in the hamlets by the road side. A month elapsed before they rejoined their battalions. Some arrived in boats on the Tagus, others on asses; nor did the whole of them return. Between Bayonne and Lisbon, the army lost seventeen hundred men, who sank under fatigue and famine, or were drowned in crossing the torrents.

The Portuguese troops were sent away from Lisbon. The first division of infantry was quartered there, not in the wretched barracks in which the native troops were lodged, but in the convents of the monks. The general of division, Delaborde, was appointed governor of the capital.

The second division, under the orders of General Loison, occupied Cintra, Mafra, and the coast as far as the mouth of the Mondego. The brigade of General Thomières was established in the fort and peninsula of Peniche, which is connected with the continent only by a slip of land that at high tides is covered with water.

The third division was appropriated to guard the entrance of the Tagus. The head-quarters of General Travot were at Oyras: he garrisoned the forts of Saint Julien and Cascaes on the right bank, and extended his force from this side to Cabo da Roca, the most westerly point of Europe. Two battalions were encamped on the left bank, on the heights of Morfacem, which command the fort of Trafaria and the tower of Bugio. This tower is built in the sea, at the extremity of a sand-bank, which is connected with the fortress of Costa. It was the object of very active vigilance, because its fire, which crosses that of Fort Saint Julien, is the main obstacle to any squadron which should attempt to force the passage of the bar of Lisbon.

The cavalry and artillery remained at Lisbon. Santarem and Abrantes were occupied, as being points proper to secure arrivals from the interior by the river. A Swiss battalion was placed in garrison at Almeida.

The General-in-chief distributed in cantonments, in the country to the north of the Tagus, the Spanish division under General Caraffa, taking care to intermix the regiments among the regiments of his own army. The two corps of that nation, which had not been put under his orders, entered Portugal in the beginning of December.

Don Francisco Maria Solano, Marquis del Socorro, presented himself on the 2nd of the month, before Elvas. This place, the bulwark of Alemtejo, was in a state to hold out a long siege. The Portuguese lieutenant-general, the Marquis d'Alorne, had thrown himself into it, after having conveyed in provisions, and reinforced the garrison with three thousand volunteers from the militia. he had been one of the first to learn of the entrance of the French into Beira; and before Solano had assembled his troops, he hastened to send to the Prince Regent, who had not yet quitted Lisbon, important information and honourable advice. His aide-de-camp, Lecor, whom he selected to bear this last homage of fidelity, returned with an order to throw open the gates of the fortress to the foreign troops. The Spanish general stationed three battalions in Elvas and its dependent forts. He established his head-quarters at Setubal, a sea-port, five leagues south of Lisbon, and from thence he sent detachments to occupy the forts and castles of Alemtejo and the Algarves.

The Spaniards were still more tardy in their invasion of the northern provinces. They passed the Minho peaceably in boats, under the cannon of Valença. This fortress, though out of repair and badly provided with artillery, is important from its position; and the Galician

Alcobaça
Memoria
Thomar
Porto de mós
Caldas
Obidos
Peniche
Berlengas
Farilhoens
Abrahão
Torres novas
Punhete
ABRANTES
S. Domingos
Carvalhal
Roliça
Rio maior
Santarem
Vimeiro
Alemquer
Chamusca
Peralles
Axeda
Almeirim
Torres Vedras
Ericeira
Mafra
Cartaxo
Villa nova
Carregado
Castanheira
Villa franca
Povoa
Muge
Ferra de Vacas
Ponte de Sor
Salvaterra
Coruche
Cintra
C. da Roca
LISBONNE
Samora Correia
S.ta Margarida
Pancas
Aldea Gallega
Lavre
Mora
Pavia
V. do Duque
Moita
Canha
Pegoens
Arrayolos
Coina
Palhota
Palmela
Setubal
Aguas de Moura
Vendas novas
Montemor novo
EVORA
C. Espichel
Saldão
Palma
Alcacer do Sal
S. Braz
Comporta
Vianna
Melides
Oudivelas
Alfundão
Grandola
S. Andre
S. Thiago
Beja
Ferreira
Alvalade
Aljustrel
Messejana
Sines
S. João
I. do Pessegueiro
S. Martinho
Entradas
Castro verde
Alcaria ruiva
Villa nova de milfontes
Ourique
S. João
S. Martinho das
Amoreiras
O Sardão
Odemira
Almodovar
Palhota
Seixes
S.ra de Monchique
Monchique
S. Marcos
Estombar
Silves
S. Braz
Arrifana
LAGOS
Alcantarilha
Villa nova
C. S. Vicente
Sagres
Albufeira
TAVIRA
Loulé
Faro
S. João
C. S.ta Maria

Coria
Hulquera
Navalmoral
Ladoeiro
Zibreira
Segura
Almaraz
Villa Velha
Coñaveral
Lugar nuevo
Monforte
Alconetar
Casas del Puerto
Montalvão
Alcantara
Garrovillas
Jaraicejo
Broxas
Cazar
Delegtosa
Nisa
Povoa
Membrio
Caceres
los Arrebatos
Carrascal
Truxillo
Castello de vide
Arroyo del puerco
Malpartida
Marvão
Benquerencia
Valencia
Aliseda
Torremocha
Conquista
Portalegre
Aldea del Cano
Castel blanco
Alegrete
Albuquerque
Casas de D.n Antonio
Montanches
Mejadas
Zorita
Villa del Rey
Navas
Val de Caballe
Arronches
de la Guia
Alcollarin
Fronteira
Campo mayor
la Roca
Aljucen
S.t Pedro
Madrigalejos
Talarubias
S.ta Olaya
Elvas
Montijo
Merida
Guadiana Fl.
Medellin
Puebla de Alcozer
Badajoz
Lobon
Talavera del Rey
Torremexia
Esparragosa
Villaviçosa
Jerumenha
Albuhera
Palomas
Cabeza del Buey
Redondo
Almendralejo
S.ta Marta
Zalamea
Olivença
Villa franca
Hornachos
Regengo
Valverde de Leganes
Feria
Fuente del Maestre
Monasterio
Belalcazar
Mourão
Barcarrota
los Santos
Zafra
la Higuera
Oliva
Xeres de los Caballeros
Llerena
As Pedras
Segura
Navafria
Moura
Frejenal
Barrancos
Cumbres
Guadalcanal
Trasierra
Higuera
Arroche
Aracena
S.ta Olalla
Casalla
Cordoue
Paimago
S.ta Barbara
Almaden
Posada
Tras la Sierra
Puebla de los Infantes
Guadalquivir
S.ta Anna
Cabezas rubias
El Ronquillo
Palma
Calañas
Lora del Rio
Puente
Palmera
S.t Lucar del Guadiana
Valverde
Guillana
la Luisiana
Ecija
Alcarias
Alcala del Rio
Carmona
Villa blanca
Santiponce
Fuentes
S.t Juan del Puerto
Niebla
Villa nueva
Seville
Marchena
Cartaya
S.t Lucar
Alcala de Guadaira
Osuna
Lucena
Manzanillas
Arahal
Moguer
Pilas
Utrera
Roda
Palos
Almonte
Montanilla
Moron
Ronda
Cabesas de la Puente
Coronil
Campillos
Torre de la Higuera
Lebrija
Puerto Serrano

corps would have been compelled to choose another debouché, had the Portuguese government manifested the slightest demonstration of hostility. The governor of Valença was Major-general Miron, an old man of eighty, formerly reputed one of the most able of the military adventurers who came, in the time of Pombal and De Lippe, to seek their fortune in Portugal. In order to remain master of the passages over the Minho and the Lima, General Taranco garrisoned Valença, and the strong castle of Sant-Jago, which commands the port of Vianna. On the 13th of December he entered Oporto, a great commercial city, the second in Portugal

It chanced that General Junot had fixed on that very day for hoisting the French tri-coloured flag at Lisbon with great pomp. It was Sunday. Six thousand infantry, cavalry, and artillery were assembled, with much parade, in the extensive square of the Rocio, to be reviewed by the general-in-chief. The populace thronged about them as they marched along, and were astonished to see them, after so short a rest, animated with that warlike gaiety which is the consciousness of courage. When the hour of twelve struck, a volley of cannon was fired from the Moor's Castle; all eyes were turned towards those old walls, which look down on the Rocio, and command the city. In an instant, the standard with the arms of Portugal, which waved on the highest of the towers, was pulled down, and in its place arose foreign colours surmounted by the imperial eagle. If there be any veteran warriors, who, after their lives have been spared by war, have dragged out existence long enough to see the banner under which their blood was shed, insulted by hostile hands, they can imagine the anguish which was now felt by the faithful sons of Lusitania. Their hearts were overwhelmed with the bitterest affliction. The fallen standard was consecrated by every remembrance of religion and of glory. In his invariable partiality for the Portuguese, Jesus Christ had given it to Alphonso-Henriquez, their first king, had impressed on it the marks of his passion, and, while confiding this second labarum to the new Constantine, had said to him, "Behold the sign under which thou shalt conquer !"

When the review was over, the troops returned to their quarters; the populace remained in the square. To the melancholy stupor with which the appearance of the foreign flag had smitten the minds of the people, succeeded, at first, confused murmurs as to the insult which had been offered to the national honour, and, next, imprecations against the French. The Marquis d'Alorne, who had arrived from Elvas, and who was probably the only one of the courtiers who was dear to the nation, happened to pass the Rocio: his name repeated, he was loudly cheered and eagerly followed. It was with difficulty that he escaped from the warm demonstrations of a popularity which was not without danger.

During the remainder of the day, the immense concourse of the people in this city, of two hundred thousand inhabitants, resembled the billows of the ocean when big with a storm. Some Frenchmen were insulted, others were seriously ill treated. The guards ran to arms, and fired some musket-shots. Among the crowd was heard the cry of " Portugal for ever! Death to the French!" At this moment the members of the government, and the principal persons of the kingdom, were assembled together at the house of the General-in-chief. "Woe be to you," said he, "if you dare to conspire against the army of the great Napoleon; your heads shall be responsible to me for the good behaviour of the people."

The opportunity was a favourable one to substitute feelings of terror, instead of the impression which had at first been made on the inhabitants of Lisbon by the pitiable state of the French army. The infantry was formed into masses of battalions in the open spaces of the New Town. The cavalry moved at a brisk trot along the line of quays which borders the Tagus. The trains of artillery, as they rolled along, frightened the citizens by the clattering of their equipage. The 13th of December may be said to be the day on which possession was really taken of the country. Thus in the Italian Republics of the middle age, adventurous warriors at the head of their iron-cased men at arms, rushed through the gates into a city, and, by the commanding spectacle of strength and rapidity united, beat the timid citizens under the yoke.

The English were in sight of Lisbon. On the departure of Sir Sidney Smith for Brazil, he left only five sail of the line on this station. But, in the course of a few days, a reinforcement of three ships of the line, three frigates, and several smaller vessels, arrived from England, under Vice-admiral Sir Charles Cotton, who assumed the command of the blockade of the Tagus. The constant presence of this naval force drew the attention of the French, and all their preparations for defence were exclusively made on the sea-coast.

After having formed a sort of lake, twelve or fourteen leagues in circumference, in which fleets may anchor and sail without being exposed to the cannon on the shore, the Tagus abruptly contracts before the western part of the city of Lisbon, in such a manner that it is but eight hundred and six fathoms wide between the Tower of Belem and the Old Tower, (*Torre Velha,*) which is built on the left bank, at the foot of the fortified eminence of Almada. From this spot to its influx into the sea, the river flows between two calcareous chains, of similar form, but of which the northern chain extends beyond and to the west of the southern chain. The channel is three leagues long; its average width is fourteen hundred fathoms. Both banks are lined with batteries and forts. At the mouth of the channel is the bar of Lisbon, intersected by a shelf of submarine rocks, called *os cachopos.* Of the two passes by which ships of the line enter the Tagus, the best is that which is nearest to the right bank.

The French were not ill supplied with materials for the defence of the banks of the Tagus. They had at. their disposal the *Fundicão* of Lisbon, an immense arsenal, in which is fabricated every thing that an army can want, from a cavalry saddle to a four-and-twenty pounder. The engineers repaired the dilapidated fortifications of the castles, raised and thickened the parapets, and constructed traverses in the works, and closed redoubts on the most commanding external points. In all the forts, fortlets, and batteries, which bore upon the passes, the officers of the artillery renewed all the necessary apparatus. Worm-eaten platforms and gun-carriages, which had been in use for more than a century, were replaced by new and solid ones. Mortars of a long range, which the General had ordered to be cast at the Fundicão, were placed in the entrenchments, and furnaces were also constructed for heating shot. With red-hot shot vessels might be destroyed; with shells they might be harassed at their anchorage. These instruments for the destruction of naval forces, were unusual among a people accustomed to live under the protection of England.

The marine likewise furnished its contingent towards defence. The late government had exhausted the arsenals to fit out the fleet which carried out the Court of Brazil. In the interval between the departure of the Prince Regent and the arrival of the French, the magazines had, in a manner, been given up to be plundered. The vivifying principle of the naval force no longer existed, for the officers and the major part of the sailors had departed with the emigrating squadron. The command of the maritime forces was given to the naval captain, Majendie, who accompanied General Junot to Lisbon, and who brought with him some French officers. He employed such Portuguese as were willing to continue in their civil and military functions. There were still in the Tagus twenty ships of war of various rates, some unserviceable, others left, because sailors could not be found to man them. Majendie soon fitted out the Vasco de Gama, and the Maria the First, both seventy-fours, three frigates, and seven lesser vessels. In less than a month the French were able to oppose to their enemies a small squadron, which, though not capable of venturing to sea, assisted in preventing the English from forcing the bar of Lisbon.

By the side of the imperial flag of France, in the Tagus, waved the imperial Russian flag. One of the fleets of that power, having on board six thousand five hundred troops and sailors, had quitted, during the conferences at Tilsit, the station of Tenedos, before the Strait of the Dardanelles. After having stopped some time at Corfu, it was returning to the Baltic, when the news of the impending rupture between England and Russia surprised it on its way. Vice-admiral Siniavin, its commander, succeeded in reaching the mouth of the Tagus before the English had taken their station there. On the 11th and 12th of November his ships entered the harbour of Lisbon; and when General Junot arrived, a few days subsequently, they were moored in order of battle behind the bar.

Between the French and the Russians there was a point of contact, but no community of interest and of glory. Siniavin was a Muscovite of the old stamp, who spoke no language but that of his country. His officers loudly censured what they called the infatuation of their

Emperor for Napoleon. In their opinion the rupture with England was only a slight cloud, which a wiser policy would soon dissipate. From all this, Junot might easily foresee what reliance, in the hour of danger, could be placed on the fidelity of such allies. The coincidence of the appearance of a Russian fleet with the irruption of the French, was, however advantageous to the latter in several respects. It was for a long while believed, even in Portugal, that Admiral Siniavin had come to aid the projects of Napoleon.

A few days before the invasion took place, the Portuguese regular troops, and the militia which the generals had raised in different parts of the kingdom, amounted to an effective force of six and thirty thousand men ready for action. In less than a month, this number was reduced more than one half, at first by desertion, and afterwards by the disbanding of the militia, and the profusion with which furloughs were granted to the troops of the line. There was no part of it preserved entire except the police guard, which, under the orders of the Count de Novion, a French emigrant, continued to do the duty of the city of Lisbon. What remained of the regiments of infantry and cavalry was dispersed in the provinces. The Portuguese horses were given to the French dragoons to re-mount them. The artillery reorganised its train and equipments. The equipments and arming of the troops were renewed. The pay was provided for by a loan of two millions of cruzados (five millions of francs), which was raised by the council of the government. Ten thousand barrels of flour were purchased at Cadiz, to provision the forts on the Tagus and the vessels, and to make a reserve of five hundred thousand rations of biscuit. The daily subsistence was secured, without its being necessary to resort to any extraordinary measure.

At this epoch the ties which had existed between the house of Braganza and Portugal were broken. The fidelity of the subjects had not failed to the blood of their Prince; it was quite the contrary. The royal family had deserted, and left them defenceless, in the midst of the danger. The court, and the fifteen thousand emigrants who followed it, had carried off with them more than half the circulating specie of the kingdom; for every one, in departing never to return, converted every thing that he possibly could into money. It was the general belief; that the counsellors of the government, foreseeing the catastrophe, had for many years been amassing specie in the private coffers of the Regent. On the day that he departed, there was more than ten thousand cruzadoes in the public treasury. The paper money was depreciated thirty per cent; the officers of the army had not received any pay for three months; the interest of the public debt was six months in arrear, and more than a year's salary was owing to the civil establishment, clerks, and judges.

The concentration of the troops within a circle of some miles round Lisbon, by making it more easy for the officers to superintend them, tended to diminish the effect that might be produced by the overbearing habits which are contracted by soldiers who are constantly victorious. Headstrong and erratic while in the mountains of Beira, the army, under a serene sky and at rest, recovered that mild sociability which distinguishes the French beyond all other people. The officers were lodged in the houses of the rich, and the soldiers shared, in the villages, the abode of the substantial peasant. Of all foreigners, the French are those with whom the Portuguese harmonise the best.

At Lisbon, General Junot allowed the Council of governors of the kingdom to continue as the Prince had established it; but he gave a place in its deliberations, with the title of Imperial Commissary and administrator-general of the finances, to the Consul Herman, whose probity and habits of business made him esteemed by the Portuguese. The public chests were not seized; the interest of the debt and the current salaries were paid; and the effect of this was, that the value of the paper-money rose twelve per cent. There was at first no remarkable variation in the price of commodities ; the acts relative to the higher police, the confiscation of English property, and the financial administration of the army, were the only ones which emanated directly from the military authority ; every thing else was done by the civil magistrates. The tumult of the 13th of December was nothing more than a transient cloud, and the hoisting of the French flag in the fortresses was looked upon as merely a conventional sign, intended to assert the military occupation. The internal government of the country had not undergone any change; and, as the governors of the kingdom exer

OF PORTUGAL

GENERAL VIEW OF LISBON, from near Almada.—From a drawing by William Telbin.

cised an authority which was delegated to them by the natural prince, the edifice of the Portuguese monarchy appeared to be still standing.

This state of things, however, was not to last long. Napoleon had received the news of the entrance of his army into Lisbon while he was in the heart of Italy. An imperial decree, issued at Milan, on the 23rd of December, 1807, condemned the Portuguese to pay to France a contribution of a hundred million of francs as the ransom of private property. The General-in-chief was directed to govern the kingdom as sole ruler, and in the Emperor's name. He was also ordered to despatch the Portuguese troops to France, with as little delay as possible; and at the same time the Corps of Observation of the Gironde took the name of the Army of Portugal.

On the 1st of February, 1808, amidst volleys of artillery on sea and land, and with almost regal pomp, Junot proceeded to the palace of the Inquisition, where the council of governors of the kingdom was sitting. The whole of the army stationed in Lisbon was under arms, to preserve the public tranquillity, as well as to render the solemnity more splendid. In a studied harangue, the French general informed the members of the council that their functions were at an end, and that to him alone would thenceforth belong the care of making the Portuguese happy. Some of the suppressed governors were nominated to fill secondary offices in the administration : Luuyt, a late directing commissary of the French armies, was appointed secretary of state in the war and naval departments; the imperial commissioner, Herman, had the home and financial departments;. the superintendence of the police, which Pombal's legislation had made of more consequence than any other branch of the ministry, was reserved for Lagarde, a Frenchman, whom the Emperor sent from Italy ; Viennot Vaublanc, inspector of reviews, was time government secretary. For the provinces new magistrates were created, under the title of corregidors mors; Pepin de Belle-Isle, Taboureau, and Lafont, three auditors of the council of state, were sent in this capacity to Abrantes, Oporto, and Setubal; Goguet, another Frenchman, was placed in time Algarves; José Pedro Quintella, a Portuguese, was chosen to hold this office at Coimbra. Without having any precisely defined functions, the corregidors mors were to centralise and give unity of action to the administration.

The ensigns of the invaded kingdom now entirely disappeared; the eagles of Napoleon assumed, on the public monuments, the place of the Portuguese quinas; the tribunals performed their judicial duties in the Emperor's name. All the natives were removed from the higher financial situations. To raise a contribution of a hundred millions of francs from a population of two millions of souls, stripped of colonies and foreign commerce, its only sources of wealth, it was necessary to descend to the husbandman and the mechanic; it was necessary even to lay hands on the most sacred objects of public veneration, by seizing the church plate.

Out of the capital, the new government was inaugurated under the most sinister auspices. A townsman of Mafra was condemned to death by a military commission, and was executed, for uttering invectives against the French army. A few days afterwards, a scuffle which took place in the small town of Caldas da Rainha, between a detachment of the 58th regiment and some soldiers of the second Oporto regiment, was falsely represented to the General-in-chief as a premeditated revolt, in which the country people had taken a part. The regiment of Oporto was broken and disbanded in a disgraceful manner. Six inhabitants of Caldas were shot, with a solemnity of preparation and display, which had a more painful effect on Portuguese imaginations than would have been caused by the tumultuous massacre of a whole district.

This was a warning to hasten the execution of the Emperor's orders with respect to the remains of the Portuguese army, and also to remove to a distance those individuals who, from their situation in society, could have the most influence over the nation. The latter were selected to proceed to France, for the purpose of meeting the Emperor, who, it was said, was soon to visit Spain and Portugal.

The thirty-seven regiments of horse and foot were reduced to six regiments of infantry, three of cavalry, and a light battalion and squadron. In the corps there were hardly soldiers enough remaining to complete the new arrangements. It was the Marquis d'Alorne who organised this small army of eight or ten thousand men, and to him also was given the command of it. The finishing of this task was not waited for to put the columns in motion. The first of them set off at the beginning of March for Valladolid, whence their march was directed on Bayonne. More than half the officers of the old army, and particularly those who belonged to the northern provinces, returned home, some because they could not obtain employment, others, because they would not accept it.

Among the officers who marched were those whose military characters stood highest: such were Lieutenant-general Gomez Freyre, Brigadiers Pamplona and Manuel de Souza, and Colonel Condido José Xavier. The Marquisses of Ponte de Lima, Valença, and Loulé, the Counts of Sabugal and Saint Michael, and many other fidalgoes of the highest rank, were superior officers of the regiments. Like the most elevated class of nobility in the other continental states, they were ambitious of the honour of serving under the banners of the Emperor Napoleon. The soldiers were far from displaying so much zeal, and it required nothing less than the name and authority of the Marquis d'Alorne to induce them to set out. More than two thousand of them, among whom were some of even the inferior officers, deserted in passing through Spain.

When the Portuguese troops began their march, they were between eight and nine thousand strong. More than four thousand, among whom were officers, escaped in passing through Spain, and returned home. Five or six hundred remained in the hospitals. Some were killed at the first siege of Saragossa. Only three thousand two hundred and forty soldiers arrived at Bayonne.

Napoleon reviewed them, and said to Prince Wolkonski, the Emperor of Russia's aide-de-camp, who had been sent on a mission to him —" These are natives of the south; they have energetic feelings; I shall make excellent infantry of them." A legion was formed of the Portuguese troops. General Junot was ordered to collect the deserters, and to send soldiers of the country, to complete it. This order, however, was not executed. Natives not being to be had, the legion was made up from the depots of Spanish prisoners. Repeated change was made in its organisation, till the month of November, 1813, when an imperial decree directed the disarming of all the foreign troops who were in the Grand Army, with the exception of the Poles.

The Portuguese legion was never employed altogether, but it served by detachments. Two battalions covered themselves with glory on the eve and on the day of time battle of Wagram, in the division commanded by General Oudinot. A regiment distinguished itself at the battle of Smolensko. The natives of the torrid hills of Alemtejo and Estremadura were numerous among those unfortunate beings who perished frozen amidst the ices of Moscow. These foreigners, thrown by chance under the standard of Napoleon, took as their motto:- *Vadimus immixti Danais, haud numinc ,nostro.*

Wherever they went, however, they deserved the esteem of their comrades in arms. The Emperor took good care not to send them to the Peninsula. Only a few officers received this destination, and it was without its having been sought by them; and they did all in their power to mitigate the calamities which war inflicted on the country. The French generals had the delicacy to abstain from employing them, on occasions in which they must have fought against their countrymen.

The English carried on war against the French army in Portugal, rather by receiving on board their ships, and encouraging by their emissaries, the malcontents of the country, than by the use of open force. Nevertheless, in the beginning of January, 1808, Admiral Cotton carried off a detachment of Portuguese invalids which garrisoned the Burlings, several fortified islets, which lie off Peniche, at four leagues distance: in their place he established a post of marines. A short time after this, a cutter, which had heard that the Russian fleet intended to set sail, reconnoitred the entrance of the Tagus. Under cover of the night it surprised a gun-boat, which the French had fitted out for the protection of the fishery. On the 3rd of March, at nine in the evening, two brigs and some boats filled with soldiers, made an attempt to carry by escalade the Fort of Bugio; they were discovered in time, and the cannon of the fort compelled them to retreat. The English were not more successful, on the night of the 22nd of April, in their attack on the corvette La Gavotte, commanded by Lieutenant Leblond-Plassan. Five boats endeavoured to carry the corvette by boarding, but were repulsed, with the loss of their commander and several marines and seamen, who were killed in the rigging and on the deck of the corvette. Ever after that period the French ships which guarded the passes, were surrounded at night by a netting, which rose eight feet above the deck. General Junot would have been delighted to repay the English in another manner. More than once, he pressed Admiral Siniavin, whose fleet was stronger than that of Admiral Cotton to quit the Tagus with some ships; but it was all in vain. Neither for the purposes of attack nor of defence, could the French reckon upon the aid of any force but their own.

The Spaniards, too, were in reality now allies only in name. Early in the month of March, the Court of Madrid recalled the divisions of its army which were stationed in Portugal. This gave rise to some displacement of the French troops. General Quesnel was sent from the headquarters at Lisbon to Oporto, to command in the northern provinces, but took no troops with him. The battalion of the twenty-sixth regiment of infantry, the Piedmontese legion of the south, a company of artillery, and a squadron of dragoons, marched, under Brigadier-general Maurin, to guard the coasts of the kingdom of the Algarves. A Swiss battalion was despatched to Elvas, and Colonel Miguel was appointed governor of that fortress. Other French troops were distributed in Alemtejo, and in that part of Portuguese Estremadura, which is on the left bank of the Tagus. General Kellerman took the command of them, and fixed himself at Setubal.

Before the end of the month, however, the Spanish troops received counter-orders. Those which had moved on Galicia from the north of Portugal, had already begun to pass the Minho; they returned to Oporto; and as their general, Don Francisco de Taranco, died on the 18th of January, Junot did not hesitate to place General Quesnel at the head of this army of ten thousand foreigners. He gave him instructions to keep down the Portuguese population by means of the Spanish soldiers, and, in case of need, to make use of that population against the Spanish troops.

The division of Don Juan Caraffa had not yet stirred from its cantonments in the neighbourhood of Lisbon, while, on the contrary, the corps of Solano had already withdrawn into Spanish Estremadura. The latter general wrote from Badajoz that he was ready to return; Junot, however, dispensed with his doing so, and merely asked him for four battalions, which he stationed at Setubal, under the French Brigadier-general Graindorge. Kellerman was ordered to remove his head-quarters to Elvas, that he might there keep an unsuspected watch on the measures of Solano, and the movements of his division. This distrust of the Spanish generals and soldiers, which was felt by the French, continued to increase throughout the months of April and May.

Previously, and as long as a good understanding appeared to he kept up between the cabinets of Paris and Madrid, the treaty of Fontainebleau was supposed to be in force; and though the military leaders were bound to keep it secret till its entire accomplishment, yet enough had transpired to the public to render it nowise doubtful what was the fate reserved for Portugal by France and Spain united; but the imperial decree of the 27th of December, 1807, thoroughly oppressive as it was, at least contained within it a reparatory principle. From the government of the kingdom being concentrated in the hands of the French general, the conclusion was hastily drawn, that Portugal would neither be rent into fragments, nor reduced to the humiliation of becoming once more a Spanish province. If at Lisbon and Oporto some pecuniary interests were for the moment injured by the Continental system, at least the agricultural population was no sufferer by it. There was a dislike to becoming a colony to Brazil. The provincial nobility, wedded to the soil, held the emigrants in contempt, and claimed to be the principal column of the state, far more than the nobility of the anti-chamber and the court. Philosophical ideas, imperfectly repressed by the police, and propagated in secret societies, were fermenting in the heads of the youth, and among the inhabitants of the cities. There does not exist in the peninsula a more extensive establishment for public instruction than the University of Coimbra. In its schools, and by its professors, are formed, for all Portugal, the judges, the administrators, the barristers, the physicians, the men of learning. The University of Coimbra was no less zealous than the German universities, against the superstition which withers the soul, against the despotism which destroys courage. All were ripe for political changes. The seeds of improvement, which were everywhere disseminated, only waited for the vivifying breath to awaken them into life.

The new Duke of Abrantes was perfectly convinced of this general feeling; but he had not dared to encourage it without the express orders of the Emperor. It was, besides, an arduous enterprise to renovate the destinies of a people. Junot was born with a talent for observation. In every question his piercing glance saw instantaneously where the difficulty lay. All the good that a sudden inspiration could produce might be expected from him; but nothing of that for which a methodical and continuous system of conduct is required All his valuable qualities were stifled by a fiery temper, habits of dissipation, and such an obstinate aversion to labour, that it palsied the exertions of those to whom he delegated some portions of his power.

BOOK III.

WHEN, at the close of the year 1807, twenty-five thousand Frenchmen invaded Portugal, Spain was the friend of France, and every day seemed to draw closer the ties by which the two powers were connected. It seemed as if, by flying to Brazil, the Braganzas had legitimatised the foreign occupation. The General-in-chief was quite delighted in contemplating the docility of the Portuguese; he even believed in the personal attachment of the inhabitants of Lisbon. His confidential reports, as well as his public acts, bore the stamp of this prepossession. This people," he continually said, "is easily managed. I am better obeyed here, and more expeditiously, than ever the Prince Regent was."

At Paris, the question presented itself under a less pleasing aspect. The Emperor had not foreseen the rising of Spain, because, in reality, it was his wish to improve the condition of the Spaniards. He expected the hatred of the Portuguese, because, in his eyes, this diminutive kingdom was merely an English colony, which was to be squeezed and ransomed. The pompous proclamations, issued by the General of his army, were sometimes in contradiction to this harsh policy. "Of what use is it," wrote the Minister Clarke, in his sovereign's name, to General Junot,—" of what use is it to make promises which you will not be able to perform? No doubt, nothing can be more laudable than to gain the confidence and affection of the inhabitants. But do not forget that the safety of the army is a paramount object. Disarm the Portuguese; keep a strict watch over the soldiers that have been sent home, that no daring leaders may appear, to make them the centres of insurrection in the interior. Watch, too, the Spanish troops. Guard the important fortresses of Almeida and Elvas. Lisbon is too large, too populous a city, and the population is necessarily hostile. Withdraw your troops from it. Hut them on the sea-coast. Keep them exercised, disciplined, collected in masses, instructed, that they may be always ready to fight with the English army, which, sooner or later, will be landed on the shores of Portugal."

The season for effecting a disembarkation was yet at a distance. On the other hand, imminent and unforeseen difficulties had arisen, with respect to the occupation of Spain. It was necessary to attend first to the business which was most pressing. Napoleon, therefore, ordered that four thousand men, of the army of Portugal, should proceed to Ciudad-Rodrigo, to support the operations of Marshal Bessiéres, and that four thousand more should he sent to General Dupont, to co-operate in taking possession of Andalusia.

The first detachment set out from Almeida, early in the month of June, under the orders of the General-of-division Loison. At a league and a half from that city, and at the very entrance of the Spanish territory, appears, on the flat summit of a granitic hill, the fort of

Conception, placed there like an advanced horse-sentinel to see what is going forward upon the Portuguese frontier. The French General offered to the Governor to send into the fort some companies of infantry, to assist him against the common enemies of France and Spain This singular proposal excited suspicion. In the course of the following night, the Governor, with his feeble garrison, escaped by a postern gate.

Nothing on this frontier indicated that Marshal Bessiéres might be expected to approach it. The province of Salamanca, like the other Spanish provinces, was arming to deliver Ferdinand VII. The fortress of Ciudad-Rodrigo was full of troops, and its ramparts were covered with artillery. General Loison had received instructions not to advance on Ciudad-Rodrigo, unless he could enter the place without fighting. He, therefore, halted his troops.

The second detachment had already entered Estremadura, under the orders of Brigadier-general Avril. The eighty-sixth regiment of infantry, the fourth provisional regiment of dragoons, and a train of ten pieces of cannon, were to join the legion of the South, at Mertola; this conjunct force was to descend the Guadiana in boats as far as Alcoutim, where it was to receive farther orders from General Dupont, the commander of the Andalusian expedition. Girod de Novilars, the commandant of a battalion of engineers, was sent to make preparations for embarking the troops. Musket shot were fired at him from San Lucar del

Guadiana, a Spanish town, opposite the Portuguese town of Alcoutim. The Andalusian insurrection had already spread from one place to another, to the borders of Portugal. Estremadura was also in a state of combustion. On the 30th of May, the revolution was effected at Badajoz, more actively, more furiously, than in the other cities, because the French were in the vicinity. The populace tore in pieces Count Torre del Fresno, whose only crime was his being a relation of the Prince of the Peace. Other Spaniards narrowly escaped the same fate. Després and Paulin, captains of Engineers, Captain Galbois, aid-de-camp to General Lagrange, and the auditor of the Council of State, M. Lacuée, who were passing through, on a mission to Lisbon, were shut up in prison, lucky in being thus rescued fromn the fury of the populace, who wished to murder themn.

Badajoz is the principal fortress of the South of Spain. It is situated on the left bank of the Guadiana, over which river there is a noble stone bridge; on the right bank stands the fort of San Cristoval. On the 1st of June, a Commissioner from the Junta of Seville arrived there, to organise the insurrection of Estremadura, and harmonise it with the general rising of Spain. The place was rendered in some measure defensible. Some troops were collected, and began to establish a camp, under the orders of General Don José Galleza, near the fort of San Cristoval. An appeal was published to all those who served by compulsion in the ranks of the French. The Portuguese soldiers on service, whom the new government paid badly, and the disbanded ones, who were not paid at all, hurried in crowds to Badajoz, from all quarters of Alemtejo. The Spaniards, of course, did the same, and with still greater eagerness; a squadron of Maria Louisa's hussars was the first to go over. A hundred and thirty men of the Valencian regiment of Volunteers escaped from Setubal with their colours. General Graindorge pursued them at the head of some French dragoons, but could not hinder them from accomplishing their purpose.

These partial desertions were only the prelude to a complete defection. The ten thousand Spaniards, who had entered the North of the kingdom, still occupied Oporto, under the command of a Frenchman, General Quesnel, who displayed extreme moderation in the exercise of his command. His prudent and reserved character would have inclined him to act so, even had not his insulated position rendered it absolutely necessary. Like the rest of the nation, the Spanish troops at Oporto had waited with extreme anxiety, to see what would be the result of the Emperor's policy. Like the rest of the nation, their indignation had been kindled, first, by time events at Bayonne, and, subsequently, by those of the 2nd of May. For a while, Quesnel hoped to restrain the Spanish soldiers by kind treatment, and by the example of the submission of the Portuguese inhabitants. He, however, armed and furnished with provisions the fort of San-Joao de Foz, at the mouth of the Douro, hoping to find an asylum there, with his weak

French escort, at the moment when the Spaniards should break out into revolt.

That moment was not long in coming. The Junta of Galicia was one of the first that was formed; it immediately began to play the part which belonged to it in the deliverance of Spain, from its possession of the ports of Ferrol and Corunna, its facility of communicating with England, and the circumstance of its having a brave and extremely dense population. The ten thousand Spaniards stationed in the Portuguese province of the Minho, were considered as the army of Galicia. The Junta ordered them, in the name of the captive King and the shamefully betrayed nation, to return into the province, and to bring with them, as prisoners, all the French whom they could find at Oporto, or on their way homeward. Don Domingo Bellesta, Marechal-de-camp of the engineer corps, the officer highest in rank since the death of General Taranco, caused General Quesnel to be arrested by his own guard. The French officers, clerks, dragoons, and cannoneers, were treated in the same manner. Had he been a man of any energy, Bellesta might easily have raised the population of Oporto against the French; but he had too little resolution, and too mean an appearance, to accomplish such an undertaking. He contented himself with hastily convoking the magistrates, and asking them whether they would be for Portugal, for Spain, or for France. " For Portugal !" they unanimously exclaimed; and immediately Major Raymundo Jose Pinheiro, temporary Governor of the Castle of San-Joao de Foz, hoisted the

Portuguese flag on his fort, and opened a correspondence with the English brig, the Eclipse, which was cruising off this coast; but the Spaniards departed to Galicia, taking with them their prisoners.

The magistrates, and especially the military commandant, Luiz da Oliveyra da Costa, terrified by the future responsibility which they had incurred, hastened to renew their submission to the French General-in-chief at Lisbon. The national flag was hauled down at San-Joao de Foz. Pinheiro took flight. The population had taken no part in the movement. It saved several Frenchmen from the hands of the Spaniards.

On the 9th of June, the news reached Lisbon, of the defection of the Spanish troops, and the carrying off of General Quesnel. Confident and careless in the ordinary circumstances of life, Junot was incapable of hesitation whenever there was imminent and palpable danger. At this moment he had about him, in Lisbon and its vicinity, Caraffa's division, composed of six battalions of infantry, a regiment of cavalry, and some troops of artillery, all of them excited to the same pitch as the others, by the intelligence which they received from Spain, and likewise stimulated to desert, by the numerous emissaries from Seville and Badajoz. Within twenty-four hours, the six battalions, the artillery, and the cavalry, were enveloped and disarmed by the French, some in their barracks, others in combined marches, on which they were dispatched in order to separate them. Of the whole division there escaped only a few hundred men of the regiment of Murcia, and some of Maria Louisa's hussars. The others were confined on board of vessels in the Tagus, surrounded by the French ships of war. The officers were allowed to remain at Lisbon on their parole.

This bold stroke filled the population of Lisbon with astonishment. It regarded the measure as only a just retribution for the treachery of which the Spanish troops had been guilty at Oporto. There was not a moment to be lost in turning it to account throughout Portugal. The General-in-chief thanked the magistrates and the inhabitants of Oporto, for the interest which they had taken in the fate of General Quesnel and his companions in misfortune. To Brigadier Oliveyra, who had pulled down the Portuguese standard at San-Joao de Foz, he promised that he would personally recommend him to the Emperor. The opinion of the Archbishop of Braga having a powerful influence in the North of Portugal, particular means of persuasion were employed for bringing him back to his allegiance to Napoleon. In the South, another influence was resorted to, that of the Count of Castro Marim, Monteiro Mor, who was living on his estates in the kingdom of Algarve. A commission of three judges of Lisbon was formed, to suggest to the General-in-chief the means of affording assistance to individuals of all classes, who had suffered in their fortune by the change of government. The Portuguese officers, both in service and on half pay, received in specie a third of their allowance, instead of a fifth which they had till then received, the rest being paid in paper-money, which was at a considerable discount.

While their situation was thus improved, an appearance of confidence was placed in them. They, it was said, ought to have the guarding of their own fortresses. In consequence, Major-general Antonio José Miranda Henriquez was ordered to raise, according to the ancient forms of the country, five companies of militia in the Alemtejo, to garrison Elvas. The most positive assurances were given both in public and private, and in all shapes, that the present disturbances in Spain arose from the Emperor's refusal to consent that Portugal should be dismembered. The Spaniards wished to take the Minho for the Queen of Etruria, Algarves for Godoy, and Alemtejo for themselves. Napoleon, on the contrary, was desirous that Portugal should preserve its provinces, its independence, and its splendour, under a monarch. The time was come to exert all their efforts in common against the common enemy. General Loison was on the point of marching to Oporto, with his column of troops, to support a faithful population, and protect it against the attacks which would undoubtedly be made on it from the side of Galicia.

Loison did, in fact, commence his march from Almeida, on the 17th of June, with two battalions and fifty horse. Another battalion, with a battery of artillery, set off from Torres Vedras, to join him by the high road. The whole number was eighteen hundred, and it was with this force that Loison was to occupy the great city of Oporto, guard Valença do Minho, Vianna, and the forts on the coast; and watch the land and sea frontier. On the 20th of June, he passed the Douro in boats, at

TORRES VEDRAS.—From Vivian's Scenery of Portugal and Spain.

Pezo da Regoa, and his two battalions slept in the bottom of the valley. The Douro flows between two very steep mountains; their sides, up to the summit, are covered with the vines which produce that excellent wine called port by the English, because it is from Porto that they obtain it.

The French continued their march on Amarante, on the morning of the 21st. The road ascends the mountain in zigzags, to render the declivity passable. The column had just advanced to Mezanfrio, when the rear-guard and the baggage, which had not yet left the banks of the Douro, were assailed by a discharge of musketry from among the vines, and behind the walls, and by stones hurled from the high points of the rocks. Loison halted, retraced his ground, and sent two companies of light troops to dislodge these troublesome irregulars. Some of them were taken, who had been old soldiers. They stated, that Padroès de Texeira and all the villages as far as the Serra de Marao, were full of insurgent peasantry; that the inhabitants of Amarante were preparing to defend the Tamega; that the most prudent were gone to Chaves in search of soldiers and cannon; and that the provinces of Tras-os-Montes and Entre Minho e Douro were rising in arms, and had sworn to combat against the French till death.

Loison congratulated himself on having been so precipitately attacked. What would have become of him, if the peasants had allowed him to advance from the Douro, and had then sunk the boats collected at the wine-magazine of Pezo da Regoa? It would have been madness, with two battalions, to encounter a numerous and enthusiastic population, in a difficult country, and leaving at his back a large river, flowing through a deep valley, which has no fords except during the most violent heat of summer, and, in the whole of its course through Portugal has not a single fixed point! Loison passed the night at Pezo da Regoa, and next day he recrossed the Douro.

It was now plain enough, that neither to the affection of the people for the French, nor even to the terror that their government inspired, must be ascribed the quietness with which the inhabitants of Oporto had remained passive spectators of the violence committed on Quesnel by the Spaniards. The news of that general's arrest had been instantaneously spread through the northern provinces. It was added, that Junot and his soldiers had been treated in the same manner at Lisbon, by Caraffa and his Spaniards. The feeling of national independence was immediately awakened in every bosom. It manifested itself first where the French troops had never shown themselves, and where no foreign influence excited the Portuguese to shake off the yoke.

On the 11th of June, an old man, who was more than eighty years of age, Manuel George Gomez de Sepulveda, a lieutenant-general, and formerly governor of Tras-os-Montes, led the way in proclaiming the restoration of the Prince Regent of Portugal, and summoned to arms the inhabitants of his province. Mirando do Douro, Ruyvaens, Villa-Real, Torre de Moncorvo, Chaves, Villapouca, and a hundred other towns and villages, almost at the same moment re-echoed the cries of *Viva o nosso principe! Viva Portugal! morra Junot! morra Napoleon!* Nearly the whole of the neighbouring province of Entre Minho e Douro participated in this enthusiasm. On the 17th, the Portuguese *quinas* were replaced, at Guimaraens; the cradle of that King of Portugal, for whom, according to the pious tradition, they descended of yore from heaven to the field of Ourique. Vianna, the seat of the provincial military authority, officially renounced, on the 18th, the French domination. For several days past, the Archbishop of Braga had offered, in his metropolitan church, the accustomed prayers for the royal House of Braganza.

At Oporto, the slight degree of interest which had been felt for General Quesnel and his companions in misfortune, rapidly died away. It was succeeded by a few days of quiet, and then burst forth the germ of popular irritation. Luiz d'Oliveira endeavoured to repress it. He was not attached to the French, still less was he an enemy to the family of his sovereigns. He, therefore, wrote to the Duke of Abrantes, protesting his submission to the Emperor Napoleon, at the same time that he wrote to General Bellesta, requesting that he would send a Spanish force, to second the patriotic and loyal wishes of the Portuguese. His object was merely to gain time.

Some fragments of the militia battalions of Oporto, Penafiel, and Maya, with which he endeavoured to maintain his tottering authority, were desirous of displaying their ancient standards, in the procession of Corpus Christi, which took place on the 16th of June. Luiz d' Oliveira formally prohibited them from doing so. Two days after, on the 18th, some carts were loading with bread at the military magazine. The inhabitants learned this, and said to each other that this bread had been required by the Juiz de Fora of Oliveira d'Azemeis, for a column of French troops, which was every moment expected. As the canoneers of the regiment of Vianna, who were employed in the arsenal, had not received their rations for several days, a man in the crowd exclaimed, "You see it is only for the Portuguese that no bread can be found." The multitude immediately raised the cry of—" Do not let us suffer this bread to be sent to the French." The carts were plundered of their contents. The national acclamations were heard, and were repeated by thousands of voices. The people thronged from all quarters. They hurried to the square of San Oviedo, in the most elevated part of the city. The doors of the arsenal were broken open, and muskets, powder, and cartridges, were distributed to all who asked for them. Joao Manuel de Mariz, a captain of artillery, got out four pieces of cannon; as there were no horses to draw them, the priests, the monks, and the women, harnessed themselves to them, and drew them up the heights of Villa Nova, on the other side of the Douro. More than ten thousand men were running through the streets. At the head of about twenty armed Spaniards, covered with dust, now suddenly appeared among the throng, Major Pinheiro, the first insurgent of

San-Joao de Foz, who had kept himself concealed since the departure of Bellesta. "A Spanish army is coming!" The Antelope brig approached, and seemed to intend to enter the river. "Here is an English squadron!" War-cries were intermingled with the firing of muskets. The alarm-bell was rung in all the churches. The constituted authority was impotent to repress a popular and turbulent insurrection, which was become so general. Luiz d'Oliveira was thrown into a dungeon, as a traitor to the nation. A great number of other citizens met with similar treatment, because they were reputed partisans of the foreigner. Those Frenchmen whom, only ten days before, a generous hospitality had rescued from the hands of the Spaniards, were now everywhere sought for, that they might be put to death.

The Portuguese nation is active, hasty, and clamorous; its good and bad qualities are more strikingly conspicuous in a city like Oporto, where a population of forty thousand souls is fed by an extensive commerce, and where the fine climate allows it to assemble in large bodies in the streets. As the multitude gave themselves up to excesses of all kinds, men of consequence, who at first kept in the back-ground, now felt the necessity of introducing themselves into this anarchical mass, in order to guide it. In that degree of civilisation which the Portuguese have attained, opinion has still a power which acts on men, when the power of government has ceased to exist. On the 19th, in the morning, the throngs of people were impelled to the episcopal palace. The bishop appeared in his balcony, gave his blessing, kissed the banners of the country, and said to those who bore them, "Let us go and return thanks to God." The flock followed its pastor to the cathedral church. After *Te Deum* had been sung, a Junta was proclaimed to govern Portugal, till the Prince Regent should signify his pleasure. This Junta was composed of eight members, chosen from among the clergy, the magistracy, the military, and the mass of the citizens: the Bishop was its president.

The instinct of patriotism had already supplied the want of a government. The inhabitants of Torre de Moncorvo destroyed the boats on the Douro, through the whole extent of their *comarca,* to prevent the garrison of Almeida from reaching their town. It was known that the French were in motion from that quarter. The ordenanças and some militia of Villa-Real and of Guimaraens, hurried to meet Loison, without orders, and almost without arms, the majority of them having nothing but pikes or scythes set in handles. It was they who fired the muskets and rolled down the stones at Pezo da Regoa. Their numbers swelled enormously, as soon as they saw the French repass the Douro. They hastened from all the surrounding country, and hung on the enemy's rear. Tired of these troublesome followers, Loison turned upon them at Castro-Dagro, killed some of them, and then continued his march to Almeida, by the way of Viseu and Calorico, without farther molestation.

Father Jose Joachim de l'Assomption, a monk of the order of Black Friars, marched at the head of this multitude, with his gown tucked up, and firing his musket, like the rest. Another monk, Father Jose Bernardo de Azevedo, went to Coimbra, with a party of the militia of Aveiro, and a crowd of peasants, to slaughter some French soldiers, who were in the hospital of that city. The poor filled the streets, the rich kept themselves close in their houses. José Pedro de Jesus, judge of the people, and a cooper by trade, gave a hearty reception to the insurgents, ordered a convent to be opened, in which were the pistols, sabres, and carbines, of some squadrons of cavalry that had been disbanded at Coimbra, and distributed these arms among the people. The higher class now took a part in the rising; the magistrates hesitatingly, the students of the university with fury. They became the grenadiers of the insurrection of the learned. The chemical laboratory was converted into a powder manufactory. The professor of metallurgy directed the making of cartridges, and the labours of the workshop for repairing arms. The temple of literature and science was metamorphosed into a military arsenal.

At this period the students were not numerous at Coimbra. Two days after this rising, on the 24th of June, forty of them, headed by Bernardo Antonio Zagolo, one of themselves, and leading two or three thousand peasants, fell upon a French detachment of foot, which was posted in Figueira, at the mouth of the Mondego, under the orders of Cibrao, a Portuguese engineer. The soldiers, who were taken by surprise, hastily threw themselves into the castle with their commander. The manner of making a defence, while surrounded by an insurgent population, was not then known. As there were no provisions in the fort, it soon capitulated, on condition of the troops being allowed to join the French army; but the capitulation was violated. The conquerors of Figuiera entered Coimbra in triumph with their prisoners. In the meanwhile, Sir Charles Cotton, the English Admiral, thinking that the fort of Figuiera, which commands a good anchorage and a coast easily accessible, might one time or other be useful to the projects of England, sent ashore a hundred marines to occupy it.

Success increased their boldness. Other students of Coimbra marched to Pombal, driving before them twelve or fifteen dragoons, who had been stationed at Condeixa-a-Velha, to keep open the correspondence; everywhere on the road there was nothing but fireworks, illuminations, and ringing of bells. Everywhere the standard of the Prince Regent was again raised.

At Leiria, too, the still increasing mass of the peasants compelled the citizens to declare themselves. The like happened at Thomar without the intervention of any kind of force from other quarters. Leiria and Thomar are only twenty-five leagues from Lisbon. All these movements, which were incessantly spreading, sprang, however, from the same principle, preserved the same character, and took place with the same circumstances. The first comer, a peasant, a shop-keeper, or a priest, described to his village, in ardent and enthusiastic terms, the ardour and enthusiasm of the neighbouring village. Then broke out transports of joy, and endless shouts and huzzas. All rushed to the church; the alarm bell was rung; bonfires were made; guns were fired; old cannon, which had never been discharged since the War of the Acclamation, were dug up to celebrate this new Portuguese restoration.

Meanwhile, the Corregidors, the Provedors, and particularly the Juiz de Fora, manifested uneasiness at the outset. The correspondence of the Intendant-general of the French police was so active! so prompt! so threatening! But they too were very soon borne away by the torrent of public feeling. The priests perambulated the towns and hamlets, preaching the French crusade. The disbanded officers and soldiers ran to arms, the militia resumed their uniforms, the Captain *mors* made appeals to a devotedness which outstripped even their call. Men started up everywhere; some armed with pikes, others with scythes fixed into handles; very few were furnished with muskets in a serviceable state. They were of all ranks, all professions, all ages; officers, militiamen, husbandmen, and particularly monks, who one while showing the crucifix, and another while tucking up their gowns, handling a musket, or brandishing a sword, served by their example or their advice, and filled indiscriminately, the office of missionaries, and the posts of soldiers or of leaders.

The Junta of Oporto imposed on itself the duty of giving regularity to these disorderly movements, and directing them to one common end. Its first care was to put down the popular class, or at least to preserve only as much of it as was necessary to combat the enemies of the country. The choice of the bishop to fill the office of President, was a step towards the accomplishment of this prudent plan. Don Antonio de San José de Castro was a descendant of the celebrated John de Castro who rendered the Portuguese name so renowned in India. He was a natural son of Count de Reizende, the hereditary high admiral. Neither in the minds of the nobles, nor of the people, is any idea of disgrace attached to bastardy, in a country where the reigning dynasty was founded by a bastard, by that warrior King, John the First, who usurped the throne in the interest and for the glory of his nation.

Don Antonio de San José de Castro entered the order of Saint Bruno when he was very young. His modest virtues, and the influence of his name, raised him successively to the dignity of principal superior of his order, and to the episcopal see of Oporto. His advanced age had kept him from taking a part in public affairs, especially since the entrance of the French and Spaniards into the kingdom. He did not possess that resolute will which commands, and still less had he that address which governs by means of management. Yet the reputation of his virtues, joined to his episcopal character, gave him the ascendant which was requisite to allay the effervescence of the inferior class, and to prevent the enthusiasm in favour of national independence from being mixed up with the democratic ideas which were fermenting in the heads of the enlightened classes. This ascendant served also to establish the superiority of the Junta of Oporto, and to make that superiority acknowledged on the North of the Tagus, both by the Juntas which the people had recently created, and by the old constituted authorities of the monarchy.

The Junta began by opening an intercourse with the enemies of France. The Viscount de Balsemao, the only man of title who was then in the northern provinces, was sent on an embassy to England, to obtain muskets, a supply of money, and troops. A correspondence was also entered into with the Junta of Galicia; but, while waiting for foreign succours, it was necessary to set a national army on foot. Commerce was called on for sacrifices, which it readily made, in order to prevent the re-establishment of an oppressive and impoverishing domination.

The civil organisation was only the means of bringing the military force into play. The supreme Junta called to assist it in council, Brigadier Bernardin Freire d'Andrada, and Colonel Don Miguel Pereyra Forjaz Coutinho, two officers who were considered as having great abilities in the administrative branch of warlike affairs, and who, rather than accept employment under the French, had retired to their own homes to wait for better days. All the arms which were in the public magazines, or in the hands of individuals, were collected; a train of field artillery was equipped; the horses which were fit for service were put in requisition; the pay was raised from forty to eighty reis; and the disbanded officers and soldiers of the regulars and militia received orders to proceed to the depots, where the old corps were being re-embodied. The second Oporto regiment, which still remembered the execution at Caldas, was one of the first to assemble again. The soldiers hung their standards with crape, and swore not to remove this sign of mourning, till they had avenged the death of their comrades, and washed out in French blood the insult that had been offered to the regiment.

The feelings which animated the opulent city of Oporto, and the rude peasantry of Tras-os-Montes, broke forth, at the same time, and with the same ardency, at the opposite extremity of the kingdom, on a coast inhabited by poor fishermen, among the Algarvians, who are considered as the mildest of the Portuguese. On the 16th of June, the inhabitants of time village of Olhâo had got together at the church door, and were reading the proclamation which Junot issued after his having disarmed the Spaniards. Colonel José Lopez de Souza, who, before the foreign invasion, was governor of the small fortress of Villa Real de San Antonio, tore down the placard. "Do not believe these falsehoods, my friends! the French deceive us, plunder us, degrade us. We are no longer Portuguese.... we are unworthy of the name!" This speech of the Colonel's went to the hearts of his hearers, and they would have run to arms, had there been any in the village. José Lopez set off to the English squadron, which was on the coast, and requested to be furnished with muskets; and as it was unable to supply them, he addressed himself to the Spanish Junta at Ayamonte. Before the arms arrived, the inhabitants of Olhâo embarked in their boats, rowed towards the fort of Armona, carried off two cannons from the coast battery, and then went to procure ammunition from the fort of Santo Lorenço, which defends the entrance of the bar of Faro. In the channel, between the isles and the coast, they saw three barks filled with French soldiers, who were going from Tavira to Faro. These they compelled to surrender.

The French had not more than nine hundred men in Algarve, besides some companies of the legion of the South at Alcoutim; the remainder were posted in reserve at Mertola, while a battalion of the twenty-sixth, fifty chasseurs, and fifty cannoneers, were distributed at Alcoutim, Villa Real de San Antonio, Tavira and Faro. General Maurin, who held the command in the province, was in the latter town, so ill as to be incapable of being removed. The active command was exercised by Colonel Maransin, of the legion of the South, who was at Villa Real de San Antonio, directing the construction of a battery against time Spanish town of Ayamonte, on the opposite bank of the Guadiana, when he learned the revolt of Olhâo. He immediately hurried to Faro, with two hundred French troops, and with the Portuguese cannoneers of the regiment of Algarve, on whom he reckoned as on his own soldiers. The insurgents of Olhâo endeavoured to stop his progress, but were soon dispersed. Goguet, the corregidor mor, assembled the magistrates of Faro, and represented to them the deluge of calamities which was about to burst on their country. They were seized with terror. In the meanwhile, Gaviel, a captain of artillery, held a parley with the insurgents of Olhâo. They trembled to see themselves in the open field, within reach of the French; they were, besides, all sailors and fishermen. A promise was made to them that the past should be forgotten, that they should not be disturbed in the exercise of their calling, and that they should be allowed to carry on the tunny fishery in the high seas. Lopez, who tore down the French proclamation, and Sebastiao Martin Mestre, who had commanded the party in the boats, took flight to Spain.

The report of the rising at Olhâo had, meantime, brought down from the mountains a multitude of armed peasants, anxious to participate in the glory of their fellow-countrymen on the coast. Obliged to keep the field, the French had in Faro only a working detachment of troops, attached to the depot of the legion of the South and of the twenty-sixth regiment of infantry. While the town was thus left to itself, one Bento Alvarez da Silva Canedo, a shopkeeper, mounted the belfry of the Carmelite church, and rang the alarm-bell. At this signal the populace broke forth into revolt. The Portuguese regiment of artillery joined their countrymen, and turned their arms against those whom they had hitherto obeyed. The sick general, and a hundred Frenchmen who were in the town, were given up to the English. There was now no rational motive for risking, at the distance of sixty leagues from Lisbon, a handful of French, who were at once threatened by the

Spaniards in Ayamonte, and by the English ships, which were almost always in sight. In consequence, the corps assembled at Tavira marched by Zambugal, to rejoin the main body of the legion of the South, at Mertola.

On his arrival there, Maransin, being desirous of learning how matters were going on in Portugal, sent a hundred infantry and thirty dragoons to Beja, to obtain intelligence and collect provisions.

Beja is an ancient city, restored by Julius Caesar, who gave it the name of *Pax Julia:* it contained six thousand inhabitants. The evacuation of Algarve, which they attributed to Portuguese valour, had turned their heads. They assassinated some Frenchmen; they insulted others. Foreseeing the disasters which would ensue, their Corregidor ran away. The Provedor, Francisco Pesagna, and the Juiz de Fora, Antonio Manuel Ribeire Cermesao, fell victims to the rage of the infuriated populace. The French detachment thought it adviseable to retreat. The inhabitants shouted victory, and gave themselves up to joy.

But before the day was out, Maransin arrived with the whole of the troops, about a thousand men, from Mertola. It was then four in the afternoon, and the soldiers had marched twelve leagues in ten hours; yet, inpatient to avenge the death of their comrades, they rushed on the city gates and the breaches in the old Roman walls. Berthier, a brave Commandant-of-battalion of the twenty-ninth, was slain. The rampart was scaled in ten places; the gates were broken down with hatchets. The city was sacked, and all who were found in arms were put to the sword.

The sacking of Beja took place on the 26th. Four days previously, Portuguese blood had flowed in Alemtejo, at Villa Viçoza, a small town, where the Kings of Portugal have a country-seat, and which is considered as the cradle of the Braganzas, because it was from thence that John IV. was taken, to be placed, against his will, on the throne of his ancestors. A company of the eighty-sixth regiment of foot was quartered at Villa Viçoza; all at once, without any previous signs of such an intention, without any provocation, it was attacked by the inhabitants, and obliged to take refuge in the castle. General Avril was then two leagues and a half off, with the remainder of the regiment. He marched with a demi-battalion, a squadron, and four field-pieces. The revolted populace was mad enough to resolve to fight the French. Antonio Lobo, a major of militia, stationed those who had muskets on the ramparts, the towers, and the adjoining houses. Those who were armed only with pikes, he drew up in column behind the town gate. This clever arrangement was made on the supposition that the French would advance by the Borba road: they came by the Capada road, where they were not expected. Seized with terror, the Portuguese took flight, and lost a considerable number of men, both in the town and on the Olivença road, by which they retreated.

Thus the insurrection burst forth in all quarters at once. The earth could not be stamped on without enemies to the French starting up from it. Lisbon itself experienced a shock, Lisbon, in which was accumulated the greatest portion of the imperial army.

The procession of Corpus Christi, in that capital, is considered as one of the most splendid solemnities of Catholic Europe. It traverses that magnificent part of the metropolis, raised by the genius of Pombal on the site of the paltry dwellings which were overthrown by the earthquake of' the year 1755. The streets are then strewed with flowers; the walls are hung with silk and embroidery; the balconies are adorned by the most beautiful, the richest, the most superbly-dressed females, who never miss this opportunity of satisfying, at the same time, a religious duty and a feeling of vanity. The procession is opened by a figure of Saint George, glittering with topazes, emeralds, and diamonds, mounted on a pal-frey of the purest white, and followed by all the retinue of the King's household. Throngs of penitents of all colours, and monks of all descriptions, form a lengthened train, which is several hours in passing by. The corporations of arts and trades, the senate, the tribunals, the councils, the regular troops, the generals, the militia come next in succession. The knights of all the orders, in their mantles and gala robes, precede the canopy, which is borne over the consecrated host. Around the canopy march a numerous clergy, and the chapter of the patriarchal church, dressed in similar robes, and equal in pomp to the college of cardinals. The sovereign, the princes of his family, and the grandees, bring up the rear of the procession on foot, without guards, and, as it were, mixed with the crowd. In peaceable times, this solemnity occasioned extraordinary precautions to be taken by the police, in consequence of the immense concourse of people which it drew to Lisbon. History has preserved the remembrance of attempts made of old by the Spaniards to assassinate King John IV. at the procession of Corpus Christi. On one occasion, during the French Revolution, Manrique, the Superintendant-of-police, stopped the Prince Regent as he was about to enter the church, by telling him that mines had been formed under the streets through which the train was to pass, and that a Jacobin conspiracy was on the point of breaking out. Though this was nothing more than a clumsy falsehood, invented to terrify the Prince Regent, and secure the success of a court-intrigue, yet, on this subject, there remained in men's minds a sort of vague uneasiness, to which the present circumstances were calculated to give a greater degree of stability.

The Duke of Abrantes ordered that the procession should take place with all its accustomed splendour. On this occasion there was every thing that the people could wish for, except the Prince and St. George, whose rich dress was carried off to Brazil. The religious congregations, however, and the constituted bodies of the state, were there in their usual situations. The cannon of the castle were fired every quarter of an hour. The streets were lined by the French infantry. The cavalry was drawn up in battle array, and the artillery ready for action, in the squares. The General-in-chief would not follow the canopy, because he wished to avoid the charge, which would certainly have been brought against him, of assuming the station of the absent Prince. To receive the benediction, he went to the palace of the Inquisition, which was become the office of the general direction of the police, and is near the church where the ceremony was performed.

The procession had been in motion three hours. Those who opened the march, after having traversed Augusta Street, Commerce Square, and Goldsmiths' Street, were entering Rocio Square. The consecrated host was just being brought out of the church of Saint Dominick. All at once the most violent agitation was visible among the people. Frightful cries were heard, which were repeated throughout the city. Some exclaimed, "The earth trembles, we shall be swallowed up!" Others, "Here are the English!—they are landed, they are coming!" But the greatest number vociferated, "Portuguese, let us stand by each other! they are killing us! they are butchering us!" The streets were too narrow to contain the crowd that rushed into them. The procession was broken; monks, penitents, judges, and knights, took to their heels. The prelate who bore the host returned into the church in dismay, and hid himself in the vestry behind a screen. In a few minutes the ground was strewed with crosses, censers, banners, penitents' bags, embroidered mantles, and plumed hats.

The infantry, being ranged in a single line on each side of the street, had not solidity enough to resist the pressure of an impetuous and compact crowd. Some soldiers were thrown down; the others formed themselves into platoons; the cannoneers loaded their pieces, and lighted their matches. The cavalry drew their sabres, and advanced in the openings of the streets.

This calm demonstration of forethought and strength was sufficient to suppress the tumult, and disperse the crowd, without a single drop of blood being shed. At the very first sign of the disturbance, the General-in-chief hurried from the Palace of the Inquisition to the church, entered the vestry, seized the officiating prelate, and led him back to the altar. "What are you afraid of?" said he to the priests and nobles. "Am not I among you? Look at my soldiers; see how firm they are. Be calm and confident like them."

Junot rallied the fragments of the train, and ordered the procession to be recommenced. He followed the canopy on foot, with the members of his government and his staff officers. Twice during the march symptoms of disorder were renewed. In the adjacent streets, men of sinister countenanecs ran about yelling, to disturb the procession. It, however, was concluded with decency. On his return to his head-quarters, amidst throngs of people, the Duke again heard, and perhaps for the last time, a few voices exclaiming, "Viva o Duque de Abrantes! Viva o nosso Duque!"

JUNOT'S INVASION

At the very moment when the streets of Lisbon echoed with the cries of "The English are landing! Here are the English!" a corps of six thousand soldiers of that nation, commanded by Major-general Spencer, was advancing by sea, from Gibraltar to the mouth of the Tagus. Its approach had for some days been announced, by signals on the coast of Algarve, and the manoeuvres of Admiral Cotton's squadron indicated offensive projects. For the last fortnight the communication had been cut off with Spain, which was known to be all in combustion. Then came, one on the back ot' the other, the insurrections of Braganza, Oporto, Coimbra, Leiria, Villa Viçoza, and Beja. The ancients gave fame a hundred voices: in popular risings she has a thousand. The accounts from the North were exaggerated even to absurdity. Loison had been defeated, taken, and put in chains, by Sepulveda. Fifty thousand armed Portuguese were marching on Lisbon, followed by twenty thousand Spaniards; and, besides these, an immense number of English were disembarked in a score of different places.

There was however, in reality, quite sufficient danger to demand all the solicitude of the leader of' the French army. He requested Admiral Siniavin to send on shore, and place at his disposal, a few hundred men of the crews of his vessels; if not as an effective succour, at least to impress on the minds of the Portuguese what a close alliance there was between the French and the Russians. But the Admiral coolly replied, that his Emperor was not at war with Portugal. The Duke of Abrantes now determined to keep garrisons only in Almeida, Peniche,

Abrantes, and Elvas, and to concentrate his army round Lisbon; but, however compact this concentration might be, still it was necessary to take care not to be hemmed in with the Tagus in the rear. Before combating the popular sedition with the sword, the Duke of Abrantes tried the effect of less murderous arms against it: he caused it to be anathematised. In a charge, published by the Patriarchal Chapter, the faithful were told, that it was a crime against God to oppose the great and invincible Napoleon, a crime punishable by the greater excommunication, independent of the legal penalties to be inflicted by the temporal power. At the same time commissioners were despatched from Lisbon, to speak, on the part of the General-in-chief, the language of conciliation to the Portuguese revolters; promising that, if the people would return to obedience, every thing should be forgotten; announcing that the Emperor had remitted one-half of the war contribution, and insinuating, that even of the other half the full payment might, perhaps, not be exacted. José Diego Mascarenhas, a judge, and a native of Algarve, was chosen to perform this task among his fellow-countrymen. He was unable to proceed farther than Alcaçer do Sal, being driven hack by the fury of the population; although no one could be more fit than he
was to conciliate, in consequence of the nobleness of his character. A more important personage was sent into the North; it was Pedro de Mello Bragner, minister for the home department, and president of the supreme tribunal of Oporto. His principal influence lay in the province of the Minho, in whiclm were his family and estates. He would

infallibly have exerted that influence, to obtain his pardon from the insurgents for having, till then, appeared to make common cause with the enemies of Portugal; but he could not accomplish his design. In the neighbourhood of Leiria, the peasants arrested him, as an agent of the French, treated him in the roughest manner, and, in spite of his remonstrances, compelled him to return to Lisbon.

It was now become necessary to resort to force. Brigadier-General Margaron was despatched from headquarters with two battalions, four select companies, two squadrons, and six pieces of cannon. On the morning of the 4th of July, intelligence reached Leiria that the French were advancing, by the way of Rio Major. This was like an electric shock to the population, whose zeal was by this time beginning to abate in its enthusiasm. The magistrates and the military leaders held a council upon the occasion. The Alcade mor, Rodrigo Barba, a retired Colonel of cavalry, was appointed Governor. Isidore Dos Santos Ferreira, Colonel of the militia, harangued the soldiers. Manuel Trigueras, the Captain mor, called in time *Ordenanças* from all quarters. A solemn Te Deum was sung by the bishops. The people carried the Portuguese standard about the streets, with huzzas and continual acclamations. Their southern imaginations reproached the enemy for coming too slowly.

Night came, and courage began to cool. The governor, the bishop, the magistrates, and a great number of the heroes of the day before, took flight. There remained in the lace but a thousand unorganised men, of whom only two hundred had muskets, and not the whole of those had cartridges. About one in the afternoon the French made their appearance. Believing that he should have to contend with regular troops, Margaron formed his brigade in order of battle, with his artillery in the centre, and his wings pushed forward to the right and left, for the purpose of surrounding the city. Some musket-shots were fired, and the peasantry ran away. The French pursued them in the place, and killed all the armed men whom they could come up with; having themselves, in this affair, only one man slain, and two wounded.

From Leiria, the column of French troops proceeded to Thomar. Frightened, but not repentant, this town submitted, and obtained its pardon, through the intercession of Timnothy Verdier, a Frenchman, who had a manufactory there. It was treated with kindness.

The march of General Margaron on Leiria had for its object, not only to obtain correct ideas relative to the insurrection of the North of Portugal, but also to procure intelligence with respect to General Loison. It was known, though indistinctly, that he was still somewhere in Upper Beira. He was ordered to return to the Tagus. Twenty copies of this order were sent to him, by every mode of conveyance that could be found. Of all these messengers only one reached him.

Loison blew up a part of the walls of fort Conception. For Almeida he allotted a garrison of twelve hundred men, composed of such soldiers as seemed to be least capable of enduring fatigue. He then, on the 4th of July, began his march through the rich valleys of Cova de Beira, and the barren mountains of the comarca of Castello Branco. It was a march through an enemy's country. The towns, the villages, had all just carried into effect their revolution against the French; and, warmed by the fervour of recent emotion, the most timid fancied themselves changed into lions. At Guarda, an episcopal city, situated in a precipitous situation, which commands the circumjacent country, the inhabitants brought down from their ancient dismantled castle, an old piece of iron canuon, which had been there for centuries. They placed it in a waggon, and stationed it in the avenue by which the French approached. This impotent bravado, and a straggling fire of musketry, drew down the anger of the soldiers on their dwellings, which were plundered. Loison spared the manufacturing town of Covilhao. It was not on his road, but there issued from it armed peasants, who assassinated the unfortunate soldiers whom exhaustion, occasioned by the heat, compelled to lag behind. The inhabitants of Truidâo and the neighbouring villages had taken flight. Those of Atalaya, commanded by their rector, endeavoured to dispute the passage. Their boldness arose from the circumstance of Joas Pedro Libeira de Carvalho, the juiz de fora of Alpedrinha, being then, with the assistance of his captain mor, raising a levy in mass in the mountains, at a distance of half a league. Brigadier-general Charlaud, with two battalions, marched against this assemblage, dispersed it before he came up with it, and overtook some of the fugitives in the defilé of Alcongosta, among whom was the captain mor, who was left on the field. Severe as these lessons were, there was no reason to hope that they would produce any beneficial effect. The French met with no resistance at Sarzedas, Cartigada, Macao, and Sardao. Not that the population was less hostile, but it was less collected together, and men had not acquired boldness by communicating to each other their identity of feeling. Besides, the troops were approaching Abrantes, in which town there was a garrison. Loison's corps arrived there on the 11th of July, having lost, in this military and toilsome march, only two hundred men, in killed, wounded, and missing.

The concentration of the troops of Alemtejo on Lisbon had been effected with less bustle. The Spaniards had received reinforcements in their camp of San Cristoval, before Badajos. Don Federico Morelli, a Lieutenant-colonel, commanded there a foreign legion, composed almost wholly of Portuguese deserters. After the unfortunate combats of Villa Viçoza and Beja, he was desirous to reinvigorate the public spirit in Alemtejo, and accordingly, with two hundred men of the foreign legion, and some hussars of the Estremadura regiment, he took post at Jerumenha, a small town, situated on the right bank of the Guadiana. This was a rallying point for the zealous individuals of the province. General Kellerman, who commanded in Alemtejo, ordered this position to be reconnoitred. He also sent out several reconnoitring parties on Badajoz. A detachment of French dragoons carried off, in one instance, the Spanish main guard on the Caya. Another detachment charged a squadron of Maria Louisa, and pursued the hussars to the bridge head of the Guadiana, where a sentinel was sabred on the glacis.

Though Badajoz is looked upon as one of the best

fortresses in the South of Spain, there was a momentary intention of attempting to take it by escalade. General Kellerman, with that view, collected a number of ladders at Elvas. The French were so well acquainted with the place, that there was a reasonable hope of success. It was known that the curtains of the South fronts, near the Guadiana, were low and easily accessible. In the city there was nothing but disorder and confusion. Those who defended it had not foresight enough to anticipate a night attack on the side of the Guadiana, which was opposite to their camp of San Cristoval, in which quarter only they expected the enemy. But the order of concentration obliged Kellermann to relinquish his project. He repaired and fully armed and victualled the forts of La Lippe and Santa Lucia, on which the defence of Elvas depends. The artillery, arms, and ammunition, which were in the other places of the province, were transported thither. Then calling in the troops formerly stationed in Algarve, which, after the combat of Beja, had established themselves at Evora, he directed his course to Lisbon. The brigade of General Graindorge was the only one remaining on the left bank of the Tagus, occupying the comarca of Setubal, which forms a part of Portuguese Estremadura.

The troops of Alemtejo and Beira were scarcely returned to the Tagus before a new alarm gave occasion to a fresh expedition. To watch the English movements in the Burling Isles, some small French posts had been stationed on the opposite coast, from San Martinho to the point of Nossa Senhora de Nazareth, and some miserable batteries had been thrown up, which were served by Portuguese cannoneers. One day, the fortlet of Nazareth, which was the principal of these batteries, was taken, and twenty men came running out of breath, from San Martinho to Peniche, to announce that the Portuguese cannoneers had revolted, and that their comrades were assassinated. Peniche and its peninsula were held by Brigadier-general Thomières with a garrison which consisted of a battalion of the fifty-eighth, a detachment of artillery, and fifty dragoons. His force, therefore, was not sufficient to allow of his sending a reconnoitring party as far as Nazareth without stripping his fortress; but he proceeded to Obidos, whence he sent a conciliatory message to the Abbot-general of the Bernardines of Alcobaça, the temporal lord and spiritual father of the country, who had till then been the obsequious servant of the French. No answer was given to the message, and it produced no effect on the peasants, who assembled in arms, obstructed the bridges, and cut up the roads. English officers and soldiers were seen among them, by the emissaries of Thomières. The general wrote that ten thousand men of that nation had landed at Nazareth, and that fifteen hundred Portuguese were come from Coimbra to join them, and march together against Lisbon.

This took place a few days after Margaron had evacuated Leiria. For a month past, there had been vague rumours, relative to different expeditions which were fitting out in the English ports. Convoys of transport vessels had several times been seen to appear and disappear at the mouth of the Tagus. The Duke of Abrantes, believing in the landing of the English, immediately got ready a corps of troops to drive them into the sea, and to suppress the Portuguese insurrection; and in order to accomplish this latter purpose it was resolved, if necessary, to push as far as Oporto, and even to cross the Douro.

Thomières quitted Peniche with two battalions, to ascertain what was going on upon the coast between Peniche and Nazareth. General Kellermann marched from Lisbon, by Villa Franca and Alcoentre, on Alcobaça, with the third regiment of dragoons, a train of artillery, and General Brenier's infantry brigade, composed of the seventieth regiment of the line, and a battalion of the fifteenth light. The columns of Brigadier-general Margaron, and of the General-of-division Loison, which were come from Thomar and Abrantes to Santarem, were directed to move to Leiria.

On the approach of Thomières, the defenders of the fort of Nazareth fired several cannon-shot, and then took flight along the sea-beach, and hid themselves in the pine-forest of Leiria. The other columns met with no enemies. The landing, which had been so much talked of, was dwindled down to the sending a few small pieces of cannon from the Burlings to the mainland, by the English. There was no other Portuguese army on this point than a tumultuous assemblage of the fishermen who lived on the coast.

Ten thousand French troops were at this moment united at Leiria. Officers and soldiers were all burning with desire to march and chastise revolt at Coimbra and Oporto. Feelings of devotedness have a right to our sympathy, and those were assuredly devoted feelings which prompted a nation, at the hazard of life and property, to rise wholly, and as one man, against the invaders of its territory. Yet the Portuguese had so long fawned to the French authority, and now, not from their own impulse, but in imitation of the example of the Spaniards, they had broken out, licentious in their enthusiasm, atrocious in their revenge when they could murder without danger, and quick to fly on hearing the first muskets fired in battle. Such enemies could inspire regular troops with nothing but disgust and horror. Accordingly, in the field there was a falling off in that discipline which had done honour to the French army during the first six months of the occupation, and which was uniformly preserved in quarters. The houses whence shot had been fired were burnt; and, in the melancholy vicissitudes of a war, in which monks were seen marching at the head of battalions, there can be little reason for surprise that, in more than one instance, churches were sacked.

It was now the 18th of July. The intense heat had dried up nearly all the springs, so that not only the Mondego and the Vouga almost everywhere, but also the Douro in several places, were fordable. It would have been easy for the ten thousand men who were collected at Leiria, to carry by assault the miserable fortifications which had been hastily constructed at Coimbra and Oporto. The mere rumour of their march would have put to the rout the few and badly organised troops of the Supreme Junta. There was nothing to prevent desolation from being spread through the northern provinces of Portugal. But Junot had bowels of compassion; he was fond of the Portuguese. He judged that a sanguinary incursion would be useless to the army, since it could tend only to exasperate still more a population which was already too much so. He recalled the troops from Leiria. Four battalions, with some squadrons of cavalry and cannon, were left at Peniche, Obidos, Rio Mayor, Santarem, and Abrantes, to watch the principal passes on the right bank of the Tagus. The other troops, and particularly those which had been with General Loison, on the expeditions of the Douro and Beira, returned to Lisbon.

Their entrance into that capital produced a strong sensation. They came in boats, having embarked on the Tagus at Santarem. Almost all the inhabitants of that great city thronged to the place of landing, at Commerce Square, to satisfy themselves with their own eyes that *Manéta* (which was the name they gave to General Loison, who had lost an arm,) was not dead: as they had been repeatedly told that both the General and his troops were destroyed. To the Portuguese, ever since the executions at Caldas, Loison was the object of a special and inveterate hatred, which had not been weakened by recent events. It would he wrong to draw, from this circumstance, any rigorous conclusions against the life and character of that general-officer. The opinion which a conquered people forms of military leaders depends less on their personal dispositions, than on the nature of the warlike measures which they are commissioned to execute. Hence it is, that the name of Turenne which is religiously venerated by the French, is still held in abhorrence in the Palatinate of the Rhine; and in Catalonia, when mothers wished to quiet their noisy and crying children, it is not long since they used to say to them, Berwick's coming!"

The Duke of Abrantes reviewed the troops with great pomp, and almost immediately dispatched them to fight in

Alemtejo. At this epoch, every day came big with anxiety, and burthened with tribulation. Affairs were not settled on the North of the Tagus, and it was now necessary to recommence on the South. There was now no question of vague and unproductive operations. The least hesitation in acting according to reasons of state, would have put to hazard the safety of the French army.

In fact, not more than twenty days had elapsed since General Kellerman evacuated Alemtejo, and Alemtejo had already its army. So prompt are the people to undertake that which they wish with a firm and unanimous resolution. Spanish garrisons occupied Castello-de-Vide, and Marvâo. The foreign legion of Moretti, at Jerumenha, reckoned a thousand men under arms, and other troops from Badajoz, were stationed in reserve behind it, at Villa Real. The Portuguese militia was acting against the weak French garrison of Elvas, and invested it so closely, that Colonel Miquel, commandant of that place, going towards dusk, from the city to Fort la Lippe, fell into an ambuscade, and was mortally wounded. Troops poured in from Portalegre, Crato, Avis, Estremoz, and Montemor-Novo; some were satisfied with half pay, others would receive nothing. The Junta of Portalegre raised a battalion of volunteers, which George d'Aviles, a rich gentleman of the town, clothed and equipped at his own expense. The second infantry regiment was re-organising at Castello-de-Vide. In the castle of Estremoz was found a supply of powder, and a great number of muskets, pistols, and sabres, which the French had neglected to destroy. The Junta of that town assembled, and laboured to put upon a good footing the two disbanded regiments, the third and fifteenth. It called to its assistance the cannoneers of the third regiment of artillery, the officers of which were retained by the French in the fort of Elvas. And, that no enthusiasm or courage might be left unemployed, it created new corps of volunteers. Villa Viçoza had formed a company of Miquelets; Evora, also, had horse and foot chasseurs; and from Badajoz there arrived a field train, of five pieces of cannon and a howitzer. Beja, which had been taught by cruel experience the superiority of regular troops over disorderly masses, now organised in battalions the young men and old soldiers, and remounted the third cavalry regiment of Olivença. Lastly, eighteen hundred men of the Ordenanças, some tolerably, and some badly armed, raised in the comarca of Ourique, in the districts of Santiago and Grandola, occupied Alcacer do Sal, and lined the left bank of the Saldao, as far as to opposite Setubal. Their ardour was kept alive by the English ships cruising before that port, and by the Comus frigate, which was off Sinès, where continual landings took place, and a correspondence was kept up with the population.

This was undoubtedly no more than the outline of an army, and an imperfect outline. The organisation of it was, however, pushed on in an active and intelligent manner. There was every day an increase of numbers, of moral energy, and of physical strength. The revolters reckoned upon time near assistance of the kingdom of Algarve, which, having been freed from the French sooner than the other provinces, must consequently have re-organised more troops. Lieutenant-general Francisco de Paula Leite, who was Governor of Alemtejo before the invasion, now resumed his command. The military action was thus centralised; there remained but one step to take, to give also some degree of unity to the civil government. At Evora a Junta was formed; the presidency of which was held in common by the General and the Archbishop of the city. It styled itself the Supreme Junta on this side of the Tagus, and began to be acknowledged as such by the majority of the other Juntas. Its first act of authority was to summon round it all the organised troops in the province.

The news of the insurrection of the Tras-os-Montes and the Minho, had reached Lisbon in an indistinct, exaggerated, and half fabulous shape, because, not having occupied those provinces, the French were obliged to trust to official reports for a knowledge of what was passing in them, and when those reports failed them, they were left in as utter ignorance of every thing as if they had been a thousand leagues from the head of the government. It was not so with respect to Alemtejo, where a residence of some months had established various kinds of connection between the troops and the inhabitants. The Duke of Abrantes was informed of the springing up and progress of this new hostile force, and he saw at once the extent of the danger. If it were allowed to exist, a day would come when, the English having landed to the north of the Tagus, the French would be pressed at once on both banks of that river. The sole reason which made the Spaniards inflame and direct the rising of Alemtejo, was to bring about the prompt deliverance of their countrymen, who were crowded in the prison ships. It was necessary to march straightforward and boldly to Evora, as the arsenal of the insurrection, and the seat of its government. In consequence, Loison passed the Tagus, on the 25th of

July, at the head of eight thousand men. His corps was composed of the three battalions of the twelfth and fifteenth light, and of the Hanoverian legion, of the fifty-eighth and fifty-ninth of the line, of the fourth and fifth provisional regiments of dragoons, forming two brigades under Generals Solignac and Margaron, of a reserve of two battalions of grenadiers, led by Major Saint Claire, and of eight pieces of cannon, commanded by Colonel d'Aboville, of the Artillery.

The Junta of Evora raised the cry of alarm, and summoned to its aid all the organised troops in Alemtejo. Evora is the third city in Portugal. Its population, in ordinary times, is fifteen thousand; but it now contained more than five and twenty thousand, in consequence of the great number of men that had flocked in from the villages, to take part in the common defence. The city is situated on the last ramifications of the Serra d'Ossa, which is an aggregation of the highest points whence the waters flow, in opposite directions, towards the Guadiana, the Saldao, and the Tagus. It was inhabited of old by the Romans, who have left there some monuments of their greatness. The walls with which it was enclosed by Sertorius fell into complete ruin in the seventeenth century, and were replaced by a bastioned envelope, the construction of the French engineer Allain Mallet. Since the ancient wars with Spain, these works had ceased to be kept up, so that in many places the parapet was obliterated, and in others the masonry had fallen down. The principal breaches were hastily cleared and entrenched. Of the five city gates, four were stopped up by barricades made of earth and stones.

The corps of Loison, marching in the heat of the dog-days through the sandy plains on the left bank of the Tagus, advanced but slowly. It proceeded on the 26th to Pegoens, on the 27th to Vendas Novas, on the 28th to Montemor-Novo. At the latter place, its advanced guard fell in with a detachment of fifteen hundred Portuguese, stationed there to watch the French movements, and which fell back in disorder on the main body, after having lost a hundred men. At eight in the morning of the 29th, the French were seen ready to rush upon Evora.

At that very moment the Spanish corps from Jerumenha, three thousand strong, arrived in that city; it consisted of the foreign legion, a battalion of provincial grenadiers, and a battalion of newly raised chasseurs. The hussar regiment of Maria Louisa, and two batteries of cannon, the one served by foot artillery-men, the other by horse artillery-men, had marched in on the preceding evening. The volunteers of Estremoz, some platoons of the regiments of infantry and militia, and the Miquelets of Villa Viçoza, were the only troops which had time to obey the summons of the Junta. Portuguese and Spaniards together, with what was already at Evora, they constituted a force of five thousand men, not including the disorderly mass of those who were come to fight, though they did not belong to any of the regular corps.

The Portuguese general, Leite, and the Spanish colonel, Moretti, ranged their little army in battle on the heights, eight hundred fathoms in front of the city, from the mill of Saint Benedict, across the eminence of Saint Caetan, as far as the quinta *dos cucos,* near the old ruined castle of Evora. This position was defended by ten pieces of cannon and two howitzers. The principal force of the infantry was established on the right. The Spanish foreign legion was formed, as a reserve, behind the centre. In the rear of the left was drawn up the Spanish and Portuguese cavalry; this was almost entirely composed of officers.

About eleven o'clock, the Hispano-Portuguese artillery and sharp-shooters opened their fire, which was replied to by the artillery and sharp-shooters of the French. General Loison reconnoitred the position, and instantly adopted the only manoeuvre which could be serviceable against the kind of enemy whom he had to encounter. He sent towards the right his first brigade, ordering General Solignac to pass beyond the enemy's flank, turn round the city on the south side, keeping close to it, and extend as far as the Estremoz road. From his left, he pushed forward the fifty-eighth of Margaron's brigade on the road of Arrayolos, directing the cavalry to move onward till it joined Solignac's brigade.

The movement being commenced, the eighty-sixth regiment was formed in column and supported at a distance by the reserve, led at the charging step, by its colonel, Lacroix, against the centre of the enemy's line. The greatest part of the Portuguese infantry, composed of soldiers collected within a few days, immediately dispersed. The Spanish and Portuguese cavalry took flight, without having struck a blow, and Leite, the general-in-chief, fled into Spain along with it. Seven pieces of cannon were taken on the field of battle. The five others were conveyed to the city by the Spanish infantry, which, led by Moretti, its colonel, and by Major Don Antonio Muria Gallejo, of the foreign legion, made a better resistance than the rest.

Evora, however, still remained to be taken. Colonel Antonio Lobo rallied the fragments of the Portuguese infantry, and placed cannon in battery to defend the Rocio-gate, the only one which was not walled up. The ramparts were covered with monks, citizens, and peasants, who uttered loud yells, embarrassed each other with their pikes, and fired muskets at the French. The Spaniards, drawn up in mass in the streets, encouraged by their presence this multitude of madmen. It was soon attacked, hand to hand, by General Solignac, on the side of the old castle, and on the fronts of Elvas by General Margaron, who followed the course of the Roman aqueduct. The soldiers pressed forward in the badly repaired breaches. Some stuck their bayonets into the walls, to serve as ladders. Others got into the city through drains and old posterns. Lieutenant Spinola, of the engineers, a native of Genoa, and an officer of General Solignac's staff, were killed in the attack; Descragnolles, another aid-de-camp of that general, was wounded while performing prodigies of valour. The assailants were quickly engaged in close combat with the Spaniards, while the Portuguese fired on them from the ramparts, steeples, windows, gates, roofs, and houses. General Loison was obliged to break open with cannon-shot, and to remove by men's labour, the barricades of the gates, in order that he might send columns into the city, to support the brave men who had effected an entrance. The Portuguese lieutenant-colonel of artillery, Domingos Gallejo, was made prisoner. A great number of Spaniards escaped, who were able to reach the Estremoz road, before the French dragoons could arrive there. The Portuguese were not so lucky. They lost more than two thousand men on the field of battle, on the ramparts, and, especially, in the streets of Evora. The pillage and slaughter lasted several hours; at length, the archbishop, Father Manuel do Cenacolo Villas Boas, obtained mercy from the victor. After severely reproaching this prelate with the dreadful consequences of a revolt which his episcopal character had authorised and sanctioned, General Loison entrusted him with the administration of the city. This day, so bloody to the insurgents, cost the French a hundred men killed, and twice that number wounded.

The sacking of Evora rang throughout Lisbon; great and small, rich and poor, all were associated with the insurrection by their feelings and wishes, while waiting to bear a part in it in arms. This hostile disposition was heightened by the still increasing distress. Those inhabitants who were in easy circumstances emigrated in crowds to the provinces of the kingdom which were no longer contaminated by the presence of foreigners. Lisbon resembled a desert; no more luxury, no more carriages, no more bustle in the streets. The disturbances in the provinces had raised the price of provisions in the metropolis; orders were no longer given to the workmen. The landed proprietors had ceased to receive their rents, and the people in office their salaries. All who formerly drew their means of existence from the court, from the fidalgos, from the clergy, and from the commercial classes, all these were reduced to ask for alms: these were more than twenty thousand. The French authorities tried to put a stop to this emigration, which was far more active and contagious than the emigration to Brazil was, when

OF PORTUGAL

VIMEIRA.—From Landmann's Historical and Military Observations on Portugal.

JUNOT'S INVASION

Junot first occupied Portugal. Persons were forbidden to quit Lisbon without a passport as if it were possible to keep the inhabitants imprisoned in an immense city, which has neither walls nor gates, and of which the outskirts are scattered over the mountains and valleys, without its being possible to discover where the country begins, and where Lisbon ends. These emigrants, as had been done with respect to the first, were summoned to return by a particular day; in default of which, their property would be confiscated, and their relations imprisoned; they and their relations laughed at Junot's decree, being thoroughly convinced that, before the expiration of the alloted term, their native land would be delivered. The inhabitants of the towns and country were ordered to give up all arms in their possession ; and this tardy disarming, which was never effected except in Lisbon and the neighbouring villages, brought into the arsenal a few hundred fowling pieces, while thousands of muskets had been neglected and abandoned in the territory occupied by the insurgents. The usual bonfires and crackers before the churches on the eve of great festivals, were prohibited; and this prohibition caused it to be reported, over and over again, in every house, what numerous crackers, and what splendid bonfires had celebrated the restoration, at Oporto, at Coimbra, and in Algarve. The Lisbon official gazette was filled with accounts of the reinforcements which had entered Spain by the way of Bayonne and Catalonia, under the orders of Marshal Lannes, who was well known to the Portuguese. They were told of the victories gained by the French at Sarragossa, Valencia, and Cordova. They replied, with the Spanish gazettes, that Sarragossa held out; that Moncey had failed before Valencia; that Dupont and his army were prisoners of war; and that the same fate would befall Junot and the army of Portugal, before the French reinforcements would have time to cross the Pyrenees.

Popular passions do not long rest satisfied with wishes and hopes. After the fruitless attempt of the procession of Corpus Christi, many efforts were made to inflame the population. On Sunday, the 24th of July, at the moment when the faithful were coming out from mass, a madman showed himself at the door of one of the principal churches, armed with a pike, which was ornamented with blue and red ribands, and having round his hat the words, *Viva o Portugal! Viva o Principe Regente nosso Senhor!* A French patrol, happening to pass by, dispersed the crowd, and seized the man who had collected it together. It was discovered that he had been dressed and put forward in this manner, to produce a manifestation of public opinion: he was tried by a military commission and shot.

On the same day, there was found, upon the high altar of the patriarchal church, an egg, on the shell of which there was very distinctly written, in strong colour, *Mora os Francesos*. This prophetic egg was taken to the headquarters. The Duke of Abrantes ordered a great number of eggs to be brought before the Portuguese. On the shell of each of them was traced, with greasy matter, the inscription *Vive l'Empereur!* These eggs were then dipped into an acid. In the course of a few minutes, the inscriptions were visible, in strong colour, on all the shells, as on the patriarchal egg. The greatest publicity was given to this counter-miracle. The eggs were conspicuously placed on the high altars of all the churches in Lisbon.

It was less easy for the French to refute the irritating proclamations, which, in spite of all their vigilance, were posted up every night, in twenty parts of the city. But, to deaden the immediate effect of them, the General-in-chief calculated, and with reason, upon an occult influence, which was placed out of the sphere of action of his own police. After the French had obliterated the government, the ensigns, and almost the name, of Portugal, there was formed at Lisbon, by the exertions of the active octogenarian José de Scabra, an association, the members of which bound themselves to each other by oath, to employ their united efforts to restore the country, and to replace the family of Braganza on the throne. All that remained at Lisbon of opulent fidalgos, of officers of superior rank, and of eminent individuals of the regular and secular clergy, cagerly entered into it. There also joined it some officers of the police guard, merchants, and even Portuguese, whom their functions connected with the government of General Junot. The society became so numerous, that it was obliged to concentrate itself; and to place itself under the management of a committee, which was called the Conservative Council of Lisbon. The title alone indicated pacific Conspirators. The committee began by opening a correspondence with the English squadron, with the Russian squadron, with the leaders of the Spanish troops, and subsequently, with the chiefs of the Portuguese insurrection in the provinces. Those daring projects, which burst forth every day among men impatient of a foreign yoke, and those calmer combinations, which are justified by the disposition of the country, came equally under the consideration of the committee; and the committee never failed to thwart whatever it had not originated, and to employ the partial conspiracies in the general conspiracy which it claimed the right of directing. This general conspiracy meanwhile, bold in words and timid in actions, still went on under the eye, and sometimes under the invisible influence, of the French general. It proceeded slowly and cautiously; in a word, in a manner suited to rich and influential men, determined, sooner or later, to accomplish their purpose, and without risking their persons or their property.

It was now impossible to reckon upon the assistance, or even the neutrality, of the smallest fraction of the Portuguese nation. Some ecclesiastics of Beja, Leiria, and Evora, who, fulfilling their sublime ministry of peace, had interposed between the victors and the vanquished, and, with the view of stopping the effusion of blood, had for a moment accepted public functions from the French generals, had by that very step incurred suspicion ; and the respect which is paid to the episcopal character, did not, at a subsequent period, prevent the Archbishop of Evora from being imprisoned by order of a sub-ordinate Junta. The public hatred was, of course, still more strongly directed against such Portuguese as had committed themselves by remaining too perseveringly attached to the government and person of the Duke of Abrantes. The merchants of the French factory, which had been so long established at Lisbon, had reason to fear that they should at length suffer by the same catastrophes which, in the Spanish cities, had overwhelmed their fellow-countrymen, who were in the same situation. Some of them joined those whom commercial speculations had brought hither with the army, and formed, as guards to the General-in-chief, a fine company of horse volunteers, of which Bastiat, a Bayonne merchant, was made captain.

The garrison of Lisbon was a model of order and discipline. The general-officers let no opportunity pass of showing it to the people. It was frequently exercised in firing, in the Campo d'Ourique, the spot where it was usually assembled. The quiet of the capital was secured, as long as it contained a great number of troops. Measures were resolved on, to obtain the same degree of security, in case the army should be compelled to leave no more than one or two battalions for the defence of the metropolis.

Of the old fortifications of Lisbon, there remains nothing but the ruined and shapeless fronts on the side of Alcantara, and an antique castle in the centre of the city, which still bears the name of the Moors' Castle, because it was built during the period of their domination. It crowns the summit of the highest of the seven hills, on which, like ancient Rome, this city is seated. Its wall of masonry, thick and not terraced, is flanked only by salient towers. Its cannon closely overlook and plunge down on the most populous streets and squares. The French put it into a defensible state. Several houses, which were built against the wall, were pulled down. Thither were conveyed a supply of water, a hundred thousand rations of biscuit, and the arms, which, from time immemorial, had never been out of the arsenal. Cannon and mortars were also sent into the castle. The terrified Portuguese imagined that a shower of bombs was about to be poured down upon their dwellings.

General Junot had also an idea of establishing an entrenched camp on the bare eminence which, in the eastern part of the city, stretches from the convent of Graça, towards Nossa Senhora do Monte. It was a mere flitting idea, such as occurs to a penetrating but indolent mind. In fact, his foresight never contemplated the plan of a methodical campaign in the interior, and on the land frontier of Portugal, such as he might one day be under the necessity of making, either to wait for reinforcements, or to retreat into Spain. That campaign would have been possible, and even easy, had provisions and ammunition been stored beforehand in the fortresses of Alemtejo, and especially in Abrantes, which its admirable position behind the Zezere, and guarding both banks of the Tagus, points out as the commanding fortress of Portugal. But, according to the generally-received ideas, Portugal was in Lisbon, and Lisbon was in itself the whole of Portugal. To see the works undertaken since the arrival of time French, and which were still continued, it might have been supposed that they could not be attacked but by fleets, and that the river was the only road by which they could be reached. The moment, however, was at hand, when the fate of the country was to be decided on another field of battle.

The army was very far from dreading that combat ; it was confident in its leader, and careless of the future. The conscripts had become immured to war by their rapid campaigns against the insurgents. These insurgents, even had there been two hundred thousand of them, would never have been sufficient to overcome the twenty thousand French soldiers of Junot. This the Portuguese knew, and their earnest and constant prayers invoked an army of liberators. From the summits of all the promontories, at the mouths of the rivers, they were seen casting their eager glances over the immensity of the ocean. At last, on the 29th of July, there arrived in Mondego Bay a numerous fleet of transports, the signals and manoeuvres of which seemed to indicate that it was preparing to effect a landing. On board of that fleet was an English army.

BOOK IV.

THE campaign which we are about to narrate lasted but twenty days. it was not distinguished, among the others by the splendour of the military events, and still less by the number of soldiers which were brought into action; it will, nevertheless, be for ever memorable, as marking the commencement of a new and more animated struggle between Great Britain and France. For fifteen years the Cabinet of St. James's had ceased to send its armies to carry on a regular war upon the Continent. Reserving the English soldiers for expeditions immediately connected with the employment of its naval forces, it attacked France only by means of the wars and conspiracies which it hired against her. There would have been nothing to induce it to change this system of policy, had the Spaniards and Portuguese peaceably accepted the yoke of the Emperor Napoleon.

In the month of November, 1807, a corps of six thousand men, under the orders of Major-general Brent Spencer, was assembled at Portsmouth, for the purpose of reinforcing the English army in Sicily, which had been weakened by the recent expedition to Alexandria. It was intended also to make use of it in seizing the Portuguese and the Russian fleets, which were in the Tagus. But the departure of the Prince Regent to Brazil, and the arrival of the French at Lisbon, caused this scheme to be abandoned. Spencer's corps proceeded to Gibraltar.

This was an intermediate station between Sicily, the first object of the expedition, and Portugal, now in the hands of the French. Other French troops crossed the Pyrenees and inundated the Peninsula. The Cabinet of St. James's was far from anticipating the resistance of the Spaniards. For a moment, the corps of Spencer was destined to capture Ceuta and the other presidencies on the African coast. At the same time, embarkations of troops were making in the British ports, with the intention of sending them to Spanish America. The English had to avenge the insult which they had received at Buenos Ayres. It was also of consequence to them to deprive Spain of the assistance of her colonies, as soon as Spain had fallen under the unlimited power of France.

In the meanwhile, the English squadrons invested the Spanish Peninsula. Admiral Sir Charles Cotton, who was charged with the blockade of the Portuguese coast, kept always in sight of Lisbon, and dispatched light vessels to cruise at the mouths of the Douro and the Mondego, between the Burlings and Peniche, off Pombal and Sinès, and along the shores of Algarve. His special mission was, to rouse the country, and this he accomplished by his secret correspondence and his proclamations. Early in the month of June, 1808, the discontent of the Portuguese appearing to be on the point of breaking out into a general rising against the French army, Admiral Cotton sent for the corps of Spencer, that, in concert with him, it might carry by a sudden attack the forts on the Tagus, and the city of Lisbon, which he supposed to be stripped of troops. Spencer arrived a few days after the rising which was attempted during the procession of Corpus Christi. Finding that the French were numerous and watchful, he returned to Gibraltar.

Spain was then awakening from its long slumber. We have seen, in the fourth book, with what sympathetic effervescence its first efforts against the French were applauded at London, and with what profusion arms and money were supplied. Lieutenant-general Sir Hew Dalrymple, who commanded at Gibraltar, despatched the corps of Major-general Spencer to Cadiz, to be at the disposal of the Junta of Seville. Another corps, of nine thousand men, was hastily assembled at Cork in Ireland, intended, according to circumstances, either to second the exertions of the Spaniards, or to attack the French in the Tagus.

The command of this corps was entrusted to Sir Arthur Wellesley, the same who has since been called Lord Wellington. He was forty years of age, and of a robust frame. He was known in his own country as a man of resolution, who had been used to war on a small scale, in the Indian campaigns, while his brother, the Marquis of Wellesley, was Governor-general. He had been promoted, about two months before, to the rank of Lieutenant-general, after the short campaign of Copenhagen, in which he had distinguished himself at the head of a brigade. In his capacity of Irish Secretary of State, Sir Arthur formed a part of the ministry. He belonged, by the violence of his political principles, to the system of government of Pitt, continued and exaggerated by that statesman's successors, Perceval and Castlereagh.

The nine thousand men embarked at Cork put to sea on the 12th of July. On the 20th, they were off Corunna. The army of Galicia had recently been defeated at Rio Seco; yet the Junta of Corunna declared to General Wellesley. that it did not stand in need of the assistance of an English army. It advised him to land in Portugal, and drive the French out of that kingdom. Sir Arthur continued his voyage, He shortened sail off Oporto, and had a conference there, with the bishop and the leading men of the country, who promised to second the British troops by the co-operation of a Portuguese army, and, besides, to supply him abundantly with provisions and the means of conveyance. He, therefore, gave orders to the convoy to stop at the mouth of the Mondego. This point of disembarkation, the most suitable, both as regarded the goodness of the anchorage and the military operations which were to ensue, was suggested by Sir Charles Cotton, whose forethought had led him to occupy, with a garrison of marines, the fort of Figueira, which commands the bay. Sir Arthur proceeded to the bar of Lisbon, to concert his measures with the Admiral. From thence he sent orders to General Spencer, to sail to Figueira, where, on the 30th of July, he himself rejoined his convoy, which had arrived on the preceding evening.

Important despatches had just been received from England. Whenever fresh intelligence arrived from Spain, a fresh explosion of enthusiasm took place in London. The British cabinet perceived that it had not yet expeditions enough to satisfy the public feeling, which was in unison with the solid interests of the country. The co-operation of the active forces of England must be proportioned to the growing and unhoped-for energy of the Spanish nation. It resolved, therefore, to send to the assistance of the Peninsula all the disposable troops which were on the territory, or in the ports of England; namely, eight battalions assembled at Ramsgate, under the orders of Brigadier-general Anstruther, and five which General Acland commanded at Harwich: eleven thousand men, who were on their way home from the Baltic, led by Sir John Moore, received the same destination. These forces, joined to the two expeditions which had already sailed, and some battalions expected from Gibraltar and Madeira, would form a total of thirty-three thousand men, including the artillery and eighteen hundred cavalry. Sir Arthur Wellesley, being the junior lieutenant-general on the army list, could not retain the command in chief. This was given to Sir Hew Dalrymple, who, in his government of Gibraltar, had been on exceedingly good terms with the Spanish authorities. Lieutenant-general Sir Harry Burrard, one of the leaders of the unfortunate expedition to Ostend in 1798, was sent from England to act as second in command.

On the point of being only the third in rank, after having embarked at Cork as General-in-chief, Sir Arthur Wellesley hastened to land the troops on both sides of the mouth of the Mondego. The westerly gales, the swell of the sea, the steepness of the coast to the North near Boarcos, the shoals to the South near Lavoos, all ran counter to the impatience of the General. The disembarkation was tedious, and cost the lives of several

English sailors and soldiers. While it was executing, the Portuguese army, commanded by Bernardin Freire, arrived at Coimbra, to the number of seven thousand infantry and six hundred cavalry. This was the whole amount of organised troops that had been produced in six weeks, by the insurrection of the northern provinces, and the efforts of the Supreme Junta of Oporto. Even of these soldiers the greatest part had no muskets; these were, however, supplied by Sir Arthur Wellesley. In a conference which the English general had with the Portuguese generals, on the 7th, at Montemor-o-Velho, it was decided, that the two armies should march straight on Lisbon, while a corps, formed of the soldiers and militia of Tras-os-Montes and Beira, commanded by Major-general Manuel Pinto Bacellar, should march, by Viseu and Castello Franco, towards Abrantes, to watch the movements of the French, in case they should endeavour to retire into Spain by that route; for among the instructions given to Sir Arthur Wellesley, his government had recommended to him, in the event of his landing in Portugal, not only to drive the French from Lisbon, but also to cut off their retreat into Spain.

While this was going on, the corps of General Spencer had reached Mondego Bay, and as soon as it had effected its landing at Lavoos, the English army began its march, on the 9th of August; it consisted of thirteen thousand three hundred infantry, two hundred horse, and eighteen pieces of artillery. It had an abundance of cartridges for the infantry, and seventeen days' bread, namely three days in the soldiers' knapsacks, and the rest carried on mules. The troops arrived on the 10th and 11th at Leiria;

the Portuguese army reached that place on the 12th, coming from Coimbra, by the route of Pombal. Crowds of peasants flocked from the neighbouring villages, to satisfy themselves with their own eyes that the English were really come, and to greet them with affectionate acclamations. The enthusiasm spread rapidly to Lisbon. The greatest part of the legion of police, which had hitherto continued faithful to the French, now passed over to the insurgents. The proclamations of General Wellesley and Admiral Cotton were widely distributed, and were read with avidity. For Portugal it was the day of deliverance, and for the French the signal of the catastrophe. It had already commenced in Spain. The victory gained at Rio Seco, on the 14th, by Marshal Bessières, came like a flash of lightning to revive their hopes. But the defeat and capitulation of General Dupont at Andujar were previously known; and that well ascertained disaster, of which no doubt could be entertained, absorbed the insignificant advantages which might result from the victory. The Duke of Abrantes soon learned that King Joseph had been obliged to abandon Madrid, a few days after having made his royal entrance into it, and that the Emperor's army was retreating on the Ebro. Thus, twenty thousand French were about to be assailed by the whole Portuguese nation, by fleets, by armies, by fourteen thousand English, whom twenty thousand more were to follow; and if they endeavoured to join such of their comrades as were nearest to them, they had to march two hundred leagues through an enemy's country, to cross broad chains of mountains and wide rivers, and to fight with victorious armies. The ten thousand Greeks of Xenophon were in a less difficult situation, when, closely pursued by the hosts of the great King, they strove to return to their native land through the territories of the barbarians.

An especial duty was imposed on the French army by the opinion which it had itself formed. The General-in-chief was accustomed to consider Lisbon, and the fleet in the Tagus, as a deposit, which must not be abandoned without having previously tried the chance of a battle. Though the Emperor had not given any positive orders on this subject, either before or since the disturbances in Spain, the General looked upon himself as responsible to him for this deposit. Had any one proposed to evacuate Portugal, while there existed the slightest probability of reaching the Ebro without sustaining a considerable loss, the proposal would have been scouted by the unanimous feeling of the army. Preparations were made to march against the enemy, for the purpose of giving battle.

The French army was not concentrated. General Loison was traversing Alemtejo, and receiving there the submission of the towns which had been terrified by the defeat of the Spaniards and Portuguese at Evora. Thinking that the terror might have extended to Badajoz, he sent Major Theron, with a regiment of dragoons and two battalions of infantry, to that place, to demand the French officers who were detained there. The Governor replied, that the fury of the people would not allow him to give them up. Steps were taking to throw in some bombs, to cool this furious population, when news arrived that the English were landed. "Hurry to Abrantes," wrote the General-in-chief to General Loison;

"there is not a moment to lose. Give up all your plans, even if you should be sure of reducing Badajoz." Loison, in consequence, hastened to complete the victualling of Elvas, the command in which was given to Girod de Novillars, chief of battalion of engineers, in the place of Colonel Miquel, who had died of his wounds. Then, marching by Arronches, Portalegre, Tolosa, and Casa Branca, he arrived on the 9th at Abrantes, after having lost a considerable number of men, who expired of thirst and fatigue. From Abrantes he could, as circumstances might dictate, either move against the van of the English army, or act on its flank.

Now that the fate of the French army was on the eve of being decided upon the right bank of the Tagus, it was of consequence to be released from all uneasiness with respect to the left. The bands of the Ordenança, which were collected at Alcaçer do Sal, formed a mass more numerous than formidable, which had not been disbanded by the roar of the cannon of Evora. Sebastiao Martin Mestre, an enterprising man, directed this assemblage, and had brought to Montalvo four heavy pieces of iron artillery, which he had found at the small harbour of Melides. The English cruiser off Setubal seemed to give support to this force, and it was said to be about to be swelled to a greater magnitude by the army of Algarve, which was crossing the mountains. General Kellermann set out from Lisbon on the 11th of August, with fifty horse, drew from Setubal eight hundred men of the thirty-first and thirty-second light regiments, marched on Alcaçer do Sal, dispersed the Portuguese, whose insignificance was now obvious, returned to Setubal, evacuated the place, after having ruined the forts, batteries, and magazines, and led back the troops to the heights of Almada, leaving a slender garrison in the old and useless Castle of Palmela, which is situated on the point of a peak that towers pre-eminently over all the mountains of this part of Portugal.

The Russian fleet still kept its station at the mouth of the Tagus. General Junot supposed that the moment was at length come to conquer the immoveableness of Admiral Siniavin: he represented to him, that the question was no longer as to fighting against the Portuguese, but, in fact, against the English, with whom the Emperor Alexander was at war; and that, under the present circumstances, it was by the land campaign that the fate of the squadron would undoubtedly he decided. He conjured him to make an attempt to put to sea, in order to alarm Admiral Cotton; or, if he was determined to remain where he was, at least to land a part of his crews, that they might be employed in defending the forts on the Tagus. Siniavin obstinately turned a deaf ear to all the propositions that were made to him, declaring that he would not fight, unless the English vessels endeavoured to force the entrance of the river.

The French army, therefore, was obliged to provide by itself for the defence of the Tagus. Brigadier-general Graindorge remained to command on the left bank; the forty-seventh regiment was established in forts Bugio and Tafaria, and on board of the vessels, to assist in the defence of the pass, and in guarding the Spanish prisoners. The sixty-sixth was destined to occupy Cascaès; the legion of the South, Saint Julian ; the twenty-sixth, Belem, Bom Succèso and Ericeyra; the fifteenth of the line, Lisbon and the powder magazines near Sacavem; a depôt battalion of twelve hundred men, drawn from the whole of the army, formed the garrison of the Castle of Lisbon. The command of this great city, and of the whole defences of the Tagus, was committed to the General-of-division Travot, who had under his orders Brigadier-general Avril, Governor of the Castle, General Fresier, and the Portuguese Marechal de camp Novion, the head of that police legion, of which only a fragment of the staff was left.

Even while these dispositions were carrying into effect, the contest had begun between the French and the English. On the first intelligence of their landing, the General-in-chief had charged Delaborde, the senior general-of-division in the army, to advance against the enemy, to watch his movements, and to manoeuvre in such a manner as to retard his march, so that time might be gained for General Loison and the reserves to place themselves in line. Delaborde left Lisbon on the 6th of August, with the seventieth regiment, forming General Brenier's brigade, two squadrons of the twenty-sixth regiment of horse-chasseurs, and five pieces of artillery. General Thomières, who occupied Obidos and Peniche with the second light infantry and the battalion of the fourth Swiss regiment, was put under his orders. Colonel Vincent, commander of the engineers of the army, followed the column, with several officers belonging to that branch of the service, for the purpose of reconnoitring the country in which the army might have to fight.

COMBAT de ROLIÇA

livré le 17 Août 1808, entre l'armée Anglaise forte de 15000 hommes et la Division commandée par le Général Delaborde forte de 2200 baïonnettes

Armée Anglaise.................................A
Réserve commandée par le Brigadier-
Général Craufurd..............................B
Brigade Portugaise............................C
Général Ferguson..............................D
Général Fane..................................E
Général Nightingale...........................F
Général Hill..................................G
Position de l'armée Anglaise après
le combat.....................................A'
Général de Brigade............................M
Général de Div.ᵒⁿ Delaborde...................N
Position de l'armée Française avant
le combat....................................(a)
Position de l'armée pendant le combat..(b)
Retraite de l'armée sur Runa.............(c)
3 Comp.ⁱᵉˢ du 70.ᵉ détachées pendant le combat..d

ECHELLES
Kilomètres
Toises
Lieue d'Espagne de 8000 Varas
Lieue de Portugal
Milles Anglais

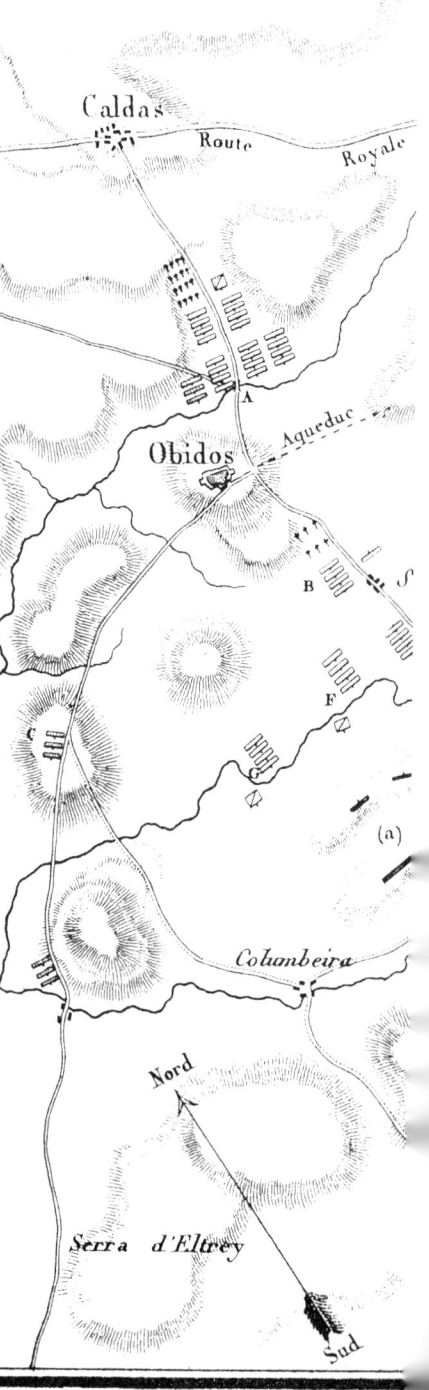

Couché fils dir.

N.º 5.

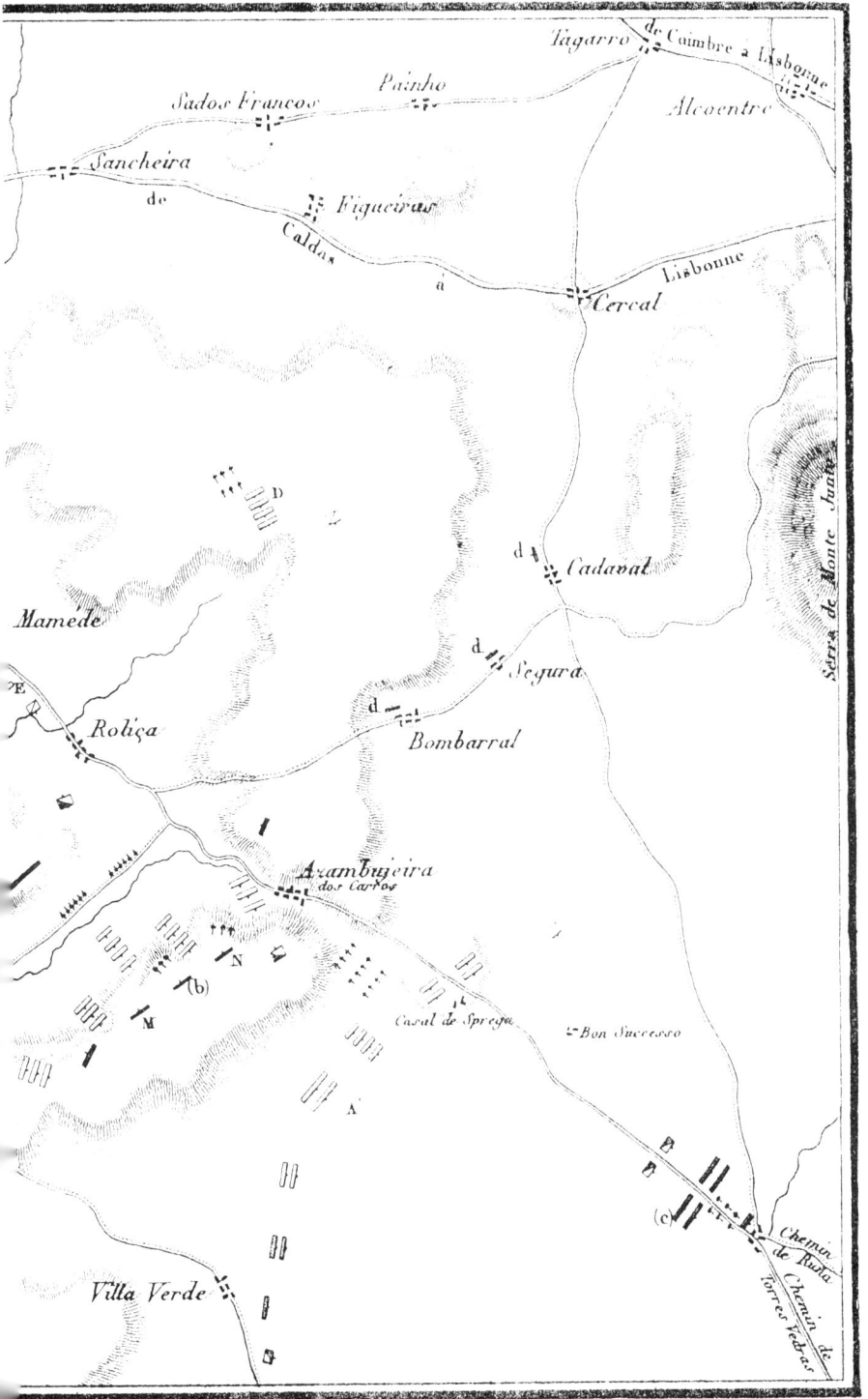

JUNOT'S INVASION

Batalha was indicated as the best point to take up for observing the English army, because it is there that the two principal communications from Lisbon to Leiria meet; namely, the royal road, which passes by Alcoentre, Rio Mayor, and Candieros, and the road nearer to the sea, which proceeds through Torres Vedras, Obidos, and Alcobaça. General Delaborde, with Brenier's brigade, followed the royal road, while Thomières' brigade marched on a line with it, by the other road. On the 11th of August, his advanced guard reached Batalha. The corps of General Loison took up its quarters at Thomar the same night.

A weak corps of troops would not have been in safety near the Abbey of Batalha, in a woody country, where it was impossible to see what was doing before it, and where nevertheless, it was approachable on all points. General Delaborde established his division at Alcobaça. On the 12th, learning that the English and Portuguese armies were united at Leiria, at the distance of a march from his camp, he fell back on Obidos, whence he despatched the fourth Swiss battalion, to garrison Peniche. On the 14th, he took up a fighting position at the village of Roliça, which is a league in the rear, leaving a battalion, as an advanced guard, near a mill, on the left of the Arnoya, and detaching three companies of the seventieth to Bombarral, Cadaval, and Segura, to connect his operations with those of General Loison, who was to be at Alcoentre on the 13th, or, at latest, on the 15th.

The English were marching by themselves, the appearance of General Loison at Thomar having so terrified the Portuguese, that they already saw the enemy arriving at Coimbra. Bernardin Freire resolved that he would not stir from Leiria, while there were any French on the other side of the Serra de Minde. Sir Arthur Wellesley easily consoled himself for being rid of allies who were somewhat too exacting, and of but little use. He asked them for fourteen hundred infantry, and two hundred-and-sixty cavalry, which he incorporated into his own army. With this reinforcement, he continued his course by the road nearest to the sea, that he might receive supplies from the fleet. Adopting the military habits of the enemy with whom he was about to contend, he left at Leiria both his baggage and his tents. The army bivouacked on the 13th at Calvaria, on the 14th at Alcobaça, on the 15th at Caldas. Four companies of riflemen, of the sixtieth German regiment, who were sent to Obidos to cover the army, pushed as far as the mill where the French advanced guard was posted. That advanced guard drove them back with loss to Obidos, and then returned in front of the village of Roliça.

The English General made no movement on the 16th, though he had reason to suppose that the troops of General Loison would join those of General Delaborde on that day, or at least on the day following.

The distance from Caldas to Roliça is three leagues; these are the northern and southern extremities of a vast bason, open equally to the west, in the midst of which stands Obidos, with its aqueduct and Moorish castle. On this side of Obidos, as you proceed towards Lisbon, the road crosses a sandy plain, covered with shrubs, till it reaches Roliça. There, from the mountains of the east, branches out a chain of small hills, bounded by the course of the waters, and stretching towards Colombeira. It seems as if all communication with the country in the rear were impracticable, because the eye entirely loses sight of the high road, near a narrow and crooked defile, which extends to Azambugeira-dos-Carros. The weak division of General Delaborde held the plain, from Roliça to as far as in front of Colombeira. At nine in the morning of the 17th, a musketry-firing was heard towards the advanced posts on the right. The English army was moving out of the passes.

It had set out, at break of day, from its camp of Caldas, formed in six columns; namely, the Portuguese brigade, which was detached to the right, to turn at a distance, by the south of Colombeira, the left of the French; four columns of the centre, one of which was in reserve, commanded by Brigadier-general Crawfurd; and three others, under the orders of Generals Hill, Nightingale, and Fane, advanced in a parallel line towards the French position, preceded by the cavalry, and protected by two batteries, each of six pieces of cannon; lastly, a strong column on the left, composed of two brigades, a battery of artillery, and a squadron of cavalry, at the head of which was General Ferguson, directed its march in such a manner, on quitting Obidos, as to outfront the enemy's right, and, if necessary, to combat with General Loison, whose corps was known to he in motion.

The English were fifteen thousand strong, and had the finest appearance. They marched slowly but with order, continually closing up the gaps which were made by the obstacles of the ground, and converging towards the narrow position of the French. In this spectacle there was something striking to the imaginations of young soldiers, who, till then, had never had to do with any thing but bands of fugitive insurgents. The French did not amount to two thousand five hundred men, including the three companies detached to the right. The flanks of the battalions were not supported by the grenadiers and light troops, these having, for the greater part, been formed into a picked regiment. The strength of this corps consisted wholly in the talents of its leaders, and especially in the coolness and energy of the General, an old warrior, beloved by the soldiers, and quick in inspiring them with his own vigour and confidence. As soon as the enemy was engaged in the plain, Delaborde judged that, if he obstinately defended Roliça, he should not leave time enough to fix himself in the strong position behind Colombeira. He sent the seventieth thither; and he himself retired to the entrance of the defile, with time second light, the artillery, and the cavalry.

This movement was executed with quickness and precision. To reach the new position of the French, which was approachable only by five ravines, with steep sides, covered by cystus, myrtle, and other shrubs, Sir Arthur Wellesley ordered five attacks. The most vigorous of these, having at the head of the column the twenty-ninth infantry regiment of Nightingale's brigade, climbed up by dint of courage and by the aid of the shrubs, and began to form on the summit. Brigadier-general Brenier charged it at the head of the first battalion of the seventieth French. The ninth English, of Hill's brigade, came to the assistance of the twenty-ninth. Colonel Lake, who commanded the attack, was killed. The two regiments were overthrown. There were even a few moments, during which the twenty-ninth laid down its arms in despair of escaping.

General Brenier dislodged, with equal success, the fifth English regiment, which attacked on the side of Colombeira. Fane's brigade, composed of the sixtieth and the ninety-fifth, endeavoured to ascend near the high road. General Delaborde repulsed them at the head of the second light; and though he had been wounded at the commencement of the action, as well as Adjutant-commandant Arnaux, the chief of his staff, and Major Merlier, of the provisional first light, he continued to hold the enemy in check, and animate his troops by his presence.

The immediate attacks of the enemy were everywhere repulsed. But the action had lasted four hours. The French had lost one fourth of their force, all killed or wounded, for they did not leave a single prisoner in the hands of the enemy, but, on the contrary, took from him more than a hundred, several of whom were officers. The English columns sent to turn the position on the right and left, were meanwhile effecting their purpose. That which Major General Ferguson commanded might reach Azambugeira dos Carros in a short time. A retreat was therefore decided upon. It was executed with a daring regularity, which, no less than the combat, excited the enemy's respect. Thrice, General Delaborde attacked the English with one half of his corps, while the other continued its retrograde movement. The twenty-sixth regiment of horse chasseurs perpetually came forward to the charge, without the Portuguese cavalry venturing to commit itself, and it several times drove the English sharp-shooters back on their masses, which were thus compelled to pause. Major Weiss, the commander of a regiment, was mortally wounded in one of these engagements. The fire of the eighteen English cannon, of large calibre, could not silence that of the five small French pieces, only one of which was left behind, embarrassed in the defile. Sir Arthur Wellesley followed the French to Cazal de Sprega. General Delaborde halted at Quinta de Maravigliata, to wait for the three companies, which, having been detached to the right on the 16th, had taken no share in the action. As soon as they rejoined him, he retired to Runa, on the Sizandro, in line with Torres Vedras. Not receiving any news there, either from General Loison, or from the Commander-in-chief, he continued his retreat on the morrow, and took post at Cabeça de Montachique, the highest point of the peninsula in which Lisbon is situated.

After the combat at Roliça, Sir Arthur Wellesley might have marched to meet General Loison, who was advancing by Rio Mayor and Alcoentre; might have driven him hack on the Tagus, crushing him by means of his superior forces, and thus have attained the purpose of the expedition, without running the risk of a battle against equal numbers. He preferred following up General Delaborde. After having spent the night of the 17th at Villa Verde, he was marching, on the morning of the 18th, on the road of Torres Vedras, when it was announced to him, that the transports from England with the brigades of Generals Anstruther and Acland on board, were in sight of the coast. The noble resistance which he had met with from General Delaborde made Sir Arthur Wellesley feel all the value of this reinforcement. He led his troops to meet it, on the road to Lourinhao. On the 19th, he took up a position at Vimeiro, so as to cover the landing which was to be effected at a league's distance, in a bay formed by the mouth of the Maceira rivulet.

Nineteen days had now elapsed, since the English began to disembark, and as yet they had only had to combat with a French advanced guard. General Loison, whose movement on Leiria had palsied the Portuguese army of Bernardin Freire, instead of advancing on Leiria or Alcobaça, had proceeded, on the 13th, by the route of Torres Novas, to Santarem. As his battalions, worn out with heat and fatigue, had left half their numbers behind, he spent the 14th and 15th in that town, to give time for the stragglers to join, which was the reason that General Delaborde fought singly at Roliça. General Loison left at Santarem the Hanoverian legion, which would have been better stationed at Abrantes, where there was an unprotected French hospital. On the 16th, being pressed by reiterated and imperative orders, he moved to Alcoentre; and, on the 17th. the General-in-chief joined him near Cercal.

The General-in-chief had also taken the field. He had quitted Lisbon for the first time since his entering it, and this he had done with extreme reluctance; not that he felt any disinclination to meeting the English in battle; on the contrary, he was resolved to fight with them. But one invariably fixed idea controlled and modified his determinations. He believed firmly, and so believed, too, the French and Portuguese who composed his government, that the quiet of Lisbon depended wholly on his presence, and that as soon as he should be at a distance from the capital, the insurrection would break out there, while, at the same time, the English squadron would force its way into the Tagus. That military combination, therefore, appeared to him to be the best, which offered the means of fighting the enemy far enough from the capital for his cannon not to be heard there, and yet near enough to allow of his return to it within forty-eight hours after the battle.

On time 15th of August, the members of the government, the heads of the clergy and of the law, and the superior officers of the army, were assembled to celebrate the Emperor's birth-day. After recommending to them to preserve the tranquillity of Lisbon, the General-in-chief the same night set off at the head of all the troops that were still disposable; namely, a regiment of grenadiers, the battalion of the eighty-second, the third provisional regiment of dragoons, and a train of ten pieces of cannon, which was followed by a supply of ammunition for the whole army, and by waggons, containing the baggage and the treasure.

This corps of troops was retarded at the passage of Sacavem, a bridge having been forgotten to be established on the river. It halted at Villa Franca da Xira. On the morning of the 17th, when it was already on its way, some Portuguese arrived from Lisbon, and announced that the English squadron had entered the

Tagus. The troops immediately retraced their footsteps. It was soon discovered that the intelligence was false, and they continued their march. The Duke of Abrantes left the direction of it to General Thiebault, the chief of his staff, and went to put himself at the head of General Loison's corps, which he met near Alcoentre, moving slowly and tardily towards Cercal.

In the meanwhile, at four leagues distance, the cannon of Roliça was distinctly heard. The peasants stated that the English army atone was engaged with General Delaborde. From these reports General Junot concluded, that, while Sir Arthur Wellesley marched on Lisbon by Torres Vedras, the Portuguese army, the strength of which was exaggerated, would proceed thither by the high road of Rio Mayor and Alcoentre. He, therefore, determined to fight the English with all his forces united, and then to return, with the same forces, against the Portuguese. From Cercal, at seven o'clock in the evening of the 17th, the General-in-chief wrote to General Thiebault: "I am collecting my army at Torres Vedras. We shall give battle to the English: make haste, if you wish to be of the party."

It was difficult to make any great haste with such a ponderous column of equipages; especially since, having quitted the royal road beyond Villa Franca da Xira, it had entered into the narrow and steep ways, which cross transversely the ramifications of Monte Junto. It arrived at La Mot-o-Otta very late on the 17th.

On the 18th, the corps of General Loison moved on Torres Vedras. The reserve slowly dragged on by Cercal, Pedromunes, and Romabhal. It extended between the van and the rear several leagues, and the most insignificant party of the enemy might have destroyed, almost without striking a blow, the equipages of the artillery, the treasures and the provisions. It did not arrive at Torres Vedras till the 20th. General Delaborde's division had returned to that place, on the 19th, from Cabeça de Montachique. A junction of all the disposable forces was thus effected.

It was now visible what a heavy tax the occupation of an enemy's country imposes on an army. According to the muster-rolls, there were, on the 15th of July, twenty-six thousand French troops in Portugal; and on the 20th of August, scarcely ten thousand bayonets or sabres could be got together on the field of battle. The marches of the month of July had occasioned a loss of nearly three thousand men, who had either fallen, or were sick in the hospitals. Five thousand six hundred were employed in occupying Elvas, Palmela, Peniche, and Santarem. Two thousand four hundred men were at Lisbon, a thousand of them on board the fleet, to guard the vessels, and keep down the Spanish prisoners; three thousand were distributed in the forts, on the two banks of the Tagus. Perceiving too late that he had retained too many fortresses, and left too many troops at the mouth of the river, the Duke of Abrantes despatched, from Torres Vedras, an order to General Travot, to send off to the army the battalion of the sixty-sixth, and four picked companies of the other battalions. Until they arrived, there were not, at Torres Vedras, more than eleven thousand five hundred men, including the non-combatants. They were formed into two divisions of

BATAILLE de VIMEIRO

livrée le 21 Août 1808 entre l'armée Anglaise forte de 20,000 hommes environ et l'armée Française forte de 9200 hommes.

ARMÉE ANGLAISE

A Position de Vimeiro, Brig.^{des} Fanes et Anstruther
B Ferguson Major général.
C Hill idem
D Craufurd id.
E Acland Brigadier général.
F Nightingale id.
G Bowed id.

ARMÉE FRANÇAISE

H Position de l'armée Française le 20 au soir.
I 1.ère Div.^{on} Général de Div.^{on}
J 2.e Div.^{on} Général de Div.^{on} Loison.
K Réserve, Général de Div.^{on} Kellermann.
L Div.^{on} de Cavalerie, Général Mageron.
M Artillerie, le Général de Brigade Taviel.
N 1.ère Brigade de la 1.ère Div.^{on} Gal Brennier.
O 1.ère Brigade de la 2.e Div.^{on} Gal Solignac.
P 2.e Brigade de la 1.ère Div.^{on} Gal Thomières.
Q 2.e Brigade de la 2.e Div.^{on} Gal Charlaud.
R 2.e Rég.^t de Grenadiers de Rés.^{ve} Colonel St Clair
S 1.er Rég.^t de Grenadiers de Rés.^{ve} Colonel Moransin.
T Cavalerie du Général Mageron
U 8.e de Dragons, Colonel Coutant
V Artillerie commandée par les Colonels Foy et Prost.
X Position des Brigades Brennier et Solignac dans leur mouvement de retraite.

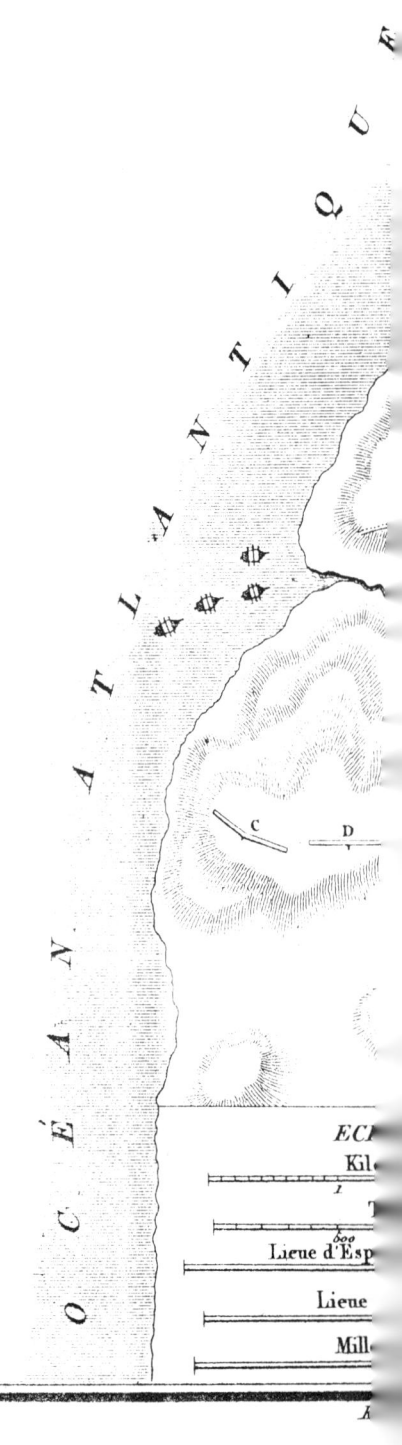

Couché fils dir.

N.º 6.

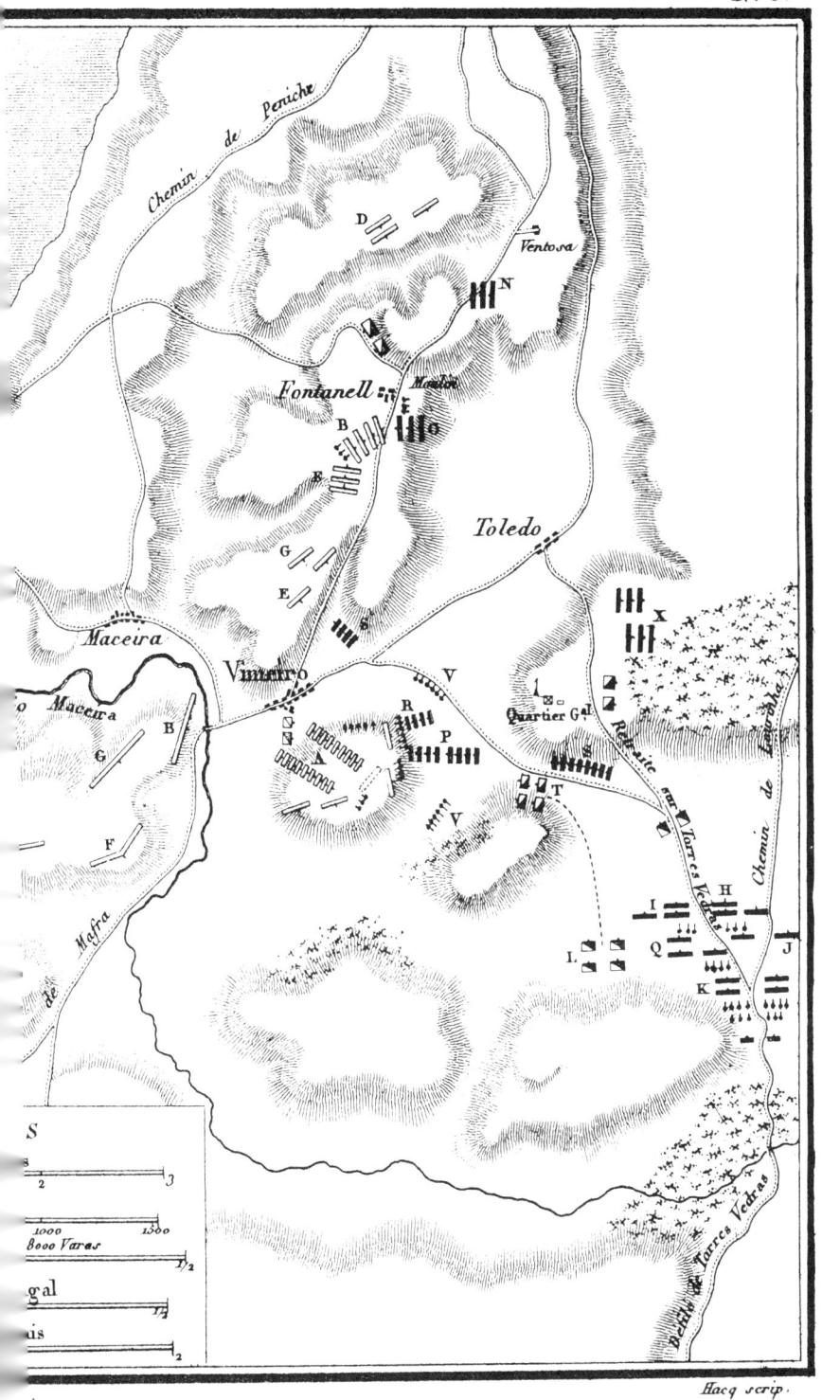

infantry, a reserve of grenadiers, and a division of cavalry.

The first division, commanded by General Delaborde, was composed of the second and fourth light, and the seventieth of the line, forming Brenier's brigade; of the eighty-sixth, and of two companies of the fourth Swiss, forming Thomières's brigade : in all, three thousand two hundred infantry.

The second division, commanded by General Loison, was composed of the twelfth and fifteenth light, and fifty-eighth of the line, forming Solignac's brigade ; of the thirty-second and eighty-second, forming Charlaud's brigade: in the whole, two thousand seven hundred infantry.

The reserve, commanded by the general of division Kellermann, consisted of four battalions of grenadiers, two regiments, making together two thousand one hundred men.

The division of cavalry, commanded by brigadier-general Margaron, consisted of the twenty-sixth horse chasseurs, and of the third, fourth, and fifth provisional regiments of dragoons, twelve hundred horse in the whole, each regiment having two squadrons.

The artillery, commanded by brigadier-general Taviel, consisted of twenty-six cannons, which were thus distributed : eight pieces in the first division, under the orders of Colonel Prost ; eight in the second division, under the orders of Colonel d'Aboville ; and ten in the reserve, under the orders of Colonel Foy.

The English outnumbered the French in the proportion of two to one. The five hundred men killed, wounded, or taken, at Roliça, were replaced, and far beyond it, by the reinforcement of four thousand two hundred men, which was brought by Generals Anstruther and Acland, and which entered into line in the course of the 20th. Besides, the station in the Burlings had made signals of the approach of the convoy from the Baltic, with eleven thousand men under Sir John Moore. Even before the landing of that force, the army, not including the Portuguese detachment, consisted of twenty-three infantry regiments (seventeen thousand men) divided into eight brigades. Having made no forced marches, it had neither sick nor stragglers. Its artillery train was four-and-twenty pieces, one battery of which was nine pounders. It was inferior to the French army only in its cavalry, which consisted of two hundred of the twentieth light dragoons, and two hundred and sixty Portuguese horse.

Without paying any attention to the force collected at Torres Vedras, the English General prepared to march by the narrow and flinty road of Mafra. This, for the space of six leagues, runs parallel to a steep coast, and forms a succession of defiles, in which the army, lengthened out in a single column, would have been perpetually assailable in rear and flank, while there was not a single spot where it could form in order of battle. But, supposing that the French would consent to remain inactive spectators of this adventurous march, Sir Arthur Wellesley would reach Lisbon some hours sooner, and General Moore would only have to move rapidly on Santarem, to cut off the retreat of the enemy into Spain.

The first part of this plan was beginning to be carried into execution.

Orders had even been issued to the troops to march on the 21st, at five in the morning ; but at that epoch, Sir Harry Burrard, who was appointed second in command of the British forces in the Peninsula, arrived in the roads of Maceira, bringing with him the chiefs of the two branches of the staff service, namely, General Clinton, Adjutant General, and Colonel Murray, Quarter-master General. Sir Arthur Wellesley went on board, to confer with his superior officer. Neither of them had any accurate ideas, either as to the force of the French army, or the difficulties of the country. The account which was given to Sir Harry Burrard, of the combat of Roliça, made him apprehend a strenuous resistance. Sir John Moore was on the point of arriving in Mondego Bay, why not wait for him? The expedition would be more certain of success, if it were undertaken with an additional eleven thousand men, and especially with a more numerous cavalry. General Burrard sent orders to Sir John Moore to land at Maceira, and directed Sir Arthur Wellesley to remain in his position of Vimeiro.

Strong positions are never wanting in irregular and mountainous countries, where cultivation has not smoothed the asperities of the ground. Vimeiro offers one of this kind, and it was formidable from the number of troops which the English had accumulated there. The village stands in the valley through which flows the Maceira. Towards the north goes off a chain of lofty knolls, along the summit of which is carried the road which passes by the hamlets of Fontanell and Ventoza, to the town of Lourinhao; this chain is bordered on the east by a large and deep ravine, at the bottom of which is the village of Toledo. To the south-east of Vimeiro, and contiguous to the houses of the village, rises a flat summit, partly wooded, and partly open, which overlooks all the avenues on the side of Torres Vedras. This flat summit is itself overlooked in the rear and to the west of Vimeiro by a mountain mass, which fills the space between the left bank of the Maceira and the sea-shore.

On this mass bivouacked six brigades of the English army, commanded by Generals Hill, Crawford, Acland, Nightingale, and Ferguson, having their advanced posts on the Mafra road. The two other brigades, Fane's and Anstruther's, were posted on the flat summit of the right bank of the Maceira. The artillery was divided between these two positions. The cavalry was left in the valley, for the convenience of obtaining water. The Lourinhao road was watched by the Portuguese and by some companies of riflemen.

This position had not been reconnoitred by the French. The detachments of their cavalry which had approached nearest to it, merely reported that the English were all concentrated round Vimeiro. and that three lines of fires had been distinctly seen during the night. But the Duke of Abrantes could not hesitate. The situation of Lisbon, abandoned to so weak a garrison, rendered him extremely uneasy. The Portuguese army was at a distance. The English, by gaining time, must grow stronger. It was necessary, then, that he should come at them, wherever they might be, and whatever their number.

JUNOT'S INVASION

On the 20th, towards evening, the French General moved his cavalry and the major part of his infantry to the junction of the Lourinhao and Vimeiro roads, beyond a long and difficult defile, which is a league from Torres Vedras. The remainder of the infantry, and the artillery, passed the defile in the course of the night. On the 21st, at seven in the morning, the French army was assembled. a league and a half from the enemy's advance posts, but out of his sight, and without his being aware of the movement.

From the point where these troops were assembled to the flat summit of Vimeiro, which the shape of the ground prevents from being seen, extends a waste of sand and rocks, which has a developement of three or four hundred fathoms, sloping down, with a rapid descent, on one side towards the ravine of Toledo on the other towards the course of the Rio Maceira. The French army moved onward, in the direction of the flat summit, the cavalry in the van, each division of infantry marching in column, with a front of two brigades, and the artillery in the interval. The third provisional regiment of dragoons, commanded by Major Contans, was sent to the right. It passed rapidly the great ravine in the vicinity of Toledo, and formed near a windmill at Fontanell, on the highest point of the road from Vimeiro to Lourinhao. This manoeuvre was seen from the English camp. General Wellesley, who was previously of opinion that his left was the weakest part of his position, was now persuaded that the attack was about to be made in that quarter. He immediately detached thither the brigade of Major-general Ferguson, with three pieces of artillery, which was followed directly in second line, by Nightingale's brigade, with two other pieces ; this latter was to be supported, still farther to the left, on the side of the sea, by Crawford's brigade and the Portuguese infantry. This movement of the English towards their left induced, on the part of the French, and as by instinct, a parallel movement. The right brigade of the second division, under the orders of General Brenier, marched, as being the nearest at hand, to succour the third regiment of dragoons.

Shortly after, the Duke of Abrantes judged that there were not troops enough on that point ; and, accordingly, the first brigade of the second division under the orders of Solignac, which followed General Brenier in the succession of columns, followed him also in his movement to the right. Six pieces of artillery of the second division likewise proceeded thither. The English General, more and more confirmed in his belief of the project which he attributed to the enemy, directed the brigades of Bowes and Acland to form in column above Vimeiro, to act as a reserve to Major-general Ferguson's detachment.

Thus it happened, that, when the sharp-shooters had scarcely began firing, there remained on the high mountain, so recently occupied by six English brigades, only three regiments of infantry, destined, under the orders of Major-general Hill, to act as a reserve to the whole army. The flat summit of Vimeiro was still crowned by the six regiments of Fane's and Anstruther's brigades, with eighteen pieces of cannon. Near half of the army was acting on the Lourinhao road, in opposition to about a third of the French army ; but with this difference in the respective positions, that the movement of the French, on their right. was made in a fortuitous manner, and was separated by a wide space of ground from their principal column, while, on the contrary the English had closed up concentrically, and the five regiments, led by Brigadiers Bowes and Acland, were so disposed as to support at once the movement of General Ferguson and the defence of Vimeiro.

The principal French column continued to proceed in its first direction. The position of Vimeiro wore a formidable aspect, because, between the lines of infantry, amphitheatrically disposed and bristling with artillery, which covered the flat summit, the brigade of Major-general Hill was also seen behind, like a third line, commanding the two others. This imposing sight, however, did not stop General Delaborde, who, advancing against the enemy, at the head of the eighty-sixth regiment of Thomières's brigade, with a warm fire of cannon and sharp-shooters, charged the fiftieth English regiment at the point of the bayonet. A few moments after, Generals Loison and Charlaud brought the battalions of the thirty-second and eighty-second into action, against the ninety-seventh English, which was succoured by the forty-third and fifty-second. In this attack, Adjutant-commandant Pillet and General Charlaud were wounded. The Chief-of-battalion Peytavy, of the eighty-second, fell pierced with wounds. The British army had no retreat except a precipitous coast, behind which was a turbulent sea, and yet Sir Arthur Wellesley did not feel the slightest degree of uneasiness. The position was strong, the troops were skilfully posted, and ably directed; what was still more important, they were numerous, and the assailing columns were deficient in depth.

General Kellermann's reserve of grenadiers had formed in line within two cannon-shot of Vimeiro, and the Duke of Abrantes stationed himself there, dividing his attention between General Delaborde's attack and his detachment on the right. When he saw that the brigades of the left could not carry the flat summit, he sent thither the second regiment of grenadier's. This brave corps, commanded by Colonel Saint-Clair, marched in column, by platoons, along the woody height which descends in rapid slope on the right towards the ravine through which the road passes from Vimeiro to Toledo. The attack made by the brigades of Thomières and Charlaud had then failed, and ail the efforts of the English were directed against the grenadiers. Eighteen pieces of cannon opened on them at once; and the Shrapnell-shells at the first discharge struck down the files of a platoon, and then exploded in the platoon that followed. Their fire was feebly answered by the artillery of the first division and of the reserve, which was compelled to keep in motion, that it might not embarrass the march of the grenadiers. Notwithstanding this inferiority of support, and the loss which it sustained, the grenadier regiment pushed on till it came within a hundred yards of the flat summit. At the moment of its forming for the attack, the column was assailed by the converging musketry-fire of six English regiments. Almost all the horses of the artillery and the ammunition-waggons were killed. The Colonels-of-artillery, Prost and Foy, were wounded. The first two platoons of grenadiers disappeared, as if they had been annihilated; the regiment could not form line of battle in front, and obliqueing to the right, in spite of the orders and example of the chiefs, it rushed headlong into the ravine.

General Kellermann followed with the second regiment of grenadiers, commanded by Colonel Maransin; he entered the ravine, marching direct against the brigade of General Acland. This rapid move-ment towards the English centre surprised them: apprehensive for the village of Vimeiro, they hastened to line the church-yard with infantry. The column of General Acland descended on the first regiment of grenadiers, and took it in flank; the second regiment had by this time been broken; the English cavalry, consisting of four hundred of the twentieth light dragoons and the Portuguese, charged the remnants of it, made many prisoners, among whom was the chief-of-battalion Palamede de Forbin, seized the dismounted and unharnessed cannon, and penetrated as far as the Duke of Abrantes, at the spot whence the reserve had been dispatched. But the French cavalry of General Margaron, which had been hidden by a small wood, now appeared; the General-in-chief's guard, the twenty-sixth horse-chasseurs, led by the chief-of-squadron, the Prince of Salm Salm, and the fourth and fifth dragoons, commanded by Majors Leclerc and Theron, rushed to the charge in their turn. The English and Portuguese were driven back and broken; they suffered a considerable loss, and their leader, Colonel Taylor was shot through the heart.

Almost at the same time, another combat took place on the road from Vimeiro to Lourinhao. Solignac's brigade, which, though last detached to the right, had first scaled the opposite mountain, (after having traversed Toledo,) had nearly reached Fontanel, and was not yet formed, when Major-general Ferguson came upon it with four regiments, and, supported by General Nightingale, opened on it a fire of battalions, and then charged. General Solignac was badly wounded, three pieces of cannon were immediately taken, and three more afterwards, and a great number of officers and soldiers were killed or wounded. The troops were driven back into the valley of Toledo.

But General Brenier's brigade was then forming in the rear and to the right of Solignac's brigade, towards the acclivity of Ventoso, where it was concealed from the English by the nature of the ground. It executed a change of front to the left. The thirtieth moved forward, and fell unawares on the seventy-first and eighty-second English regiments, which had halted in the bottom. The cannon were recovered. But, taking advantage of their enormous numerical superiority, the English returned to the charge in front, with six regiments of infantry, while Crawford's brigade arrived on the right, and began a fire of sharpshooters, which outflanked the French line. The artillery of the English also kept up a hot fire. The two parties came to chose quarters, and the General was wounded and made prisoner. In vain the third regiment of dragoons attempted several charges; they were rendered abortive by the roughness of the ground, and many brave officers fell, among whom was the young Arrighi, allied by blood to the Bonaparte family. The four weak battalions fell back in the ravine. This brigade and that of General Solignac were now without leaders. General Thiebault chief of the general staff, hastened to take the command. He rallied the troops, and withdrew them slowly, and by echelons, to the position in the rear of Toledo.

General Kellermann had also extricated himself from the action, at the head of the first regiment of grenadiers, which marched coolly and in close order, and was joined by the remains of the second. The division of cavalry had discontinued the pursuit. It presented two lines of battle, at six hundred fathoms from the positions of the enemy, thus affording a screen to the rallying of the infantry. It was now noon. The firing had lasted only two hours and a half, and yet every corps, every soldier, had fought, even that volunteer horse-guard, which was composed of the French merchants of Lisbon. The French had lost nearly eighteen hundred men, killed, wounded, or missing; an enormous loss with reference to their scanty numbers, and in comparison with that of the English, which did not amount to eight hundred men ; the English lost only one superior officer: their artillery was untouched. Their reserve of infantry had not been engaged. The sound of the trumpets was heard along the whole of the line. It seemed that, following the twentieth dragoons, and to repair the check which it had sustained, masses of infantry were going to descend. It was not so. Sir Arthur Wellesley had forbidden the troops to quit their posts without orders from him. Not a battalion stirred, even the sharp-shooters ceased their fire, and remained as though they had been vanquished.

It was Sir Arthur Wellesley who commanded in this battle. Lieutenant-General Sir Harry Burrard did, indeed, arrive on the ground during the attack on the flat summit of Vimeiro, but he left to his junior comrade the task of terminating an action which had been so auspiciously begun. The latter suffered the precise moment to escape, in which he might have pursued or crushed his enemy. The French army was soon in a posture for action again. About two o'clock arrived from Lisbon a battalion of the sixty-sixth, and the picked companies of the Hanoverian legion, and of the legion of the South. This reinforcement partly filled up the void which the battle had made. Some pieces of cannon, dismounted in the attack on the flat summit, were lying on the ground, as if to invite those who were nearest to come and take them. But the English resisted the temptation. They were not desirous to change a well-managed defence, into a battle of which the issue appeared to them to be doubtful. Tired of waiting for them, the French army repassed the *defilé* towards evening, and returned to Torres Vedras.

On the morning of the 22nd, the Duke of Abrantes convoked to a council of war, at Torres Vedras. the generals of division, Delaborde, Loison, and Kellermann, Brigadier-General Thiebault, chief of the general staff, Brigadier-General Taviel, commandant of artillery, Colonel Vincent, commandant of engineers, and Trousset, the chief intendant commissary. He laid before them the situation of the army. It had fought on the day before, rather to fulfil an honourable duty, than in the hope of being victorious. From the prisoners it was known, that the English army was about to receive reinforcements, which would raise it to double its actual number. Other reports announced, that the Portuguese army, under Bernardin Freire, had been for two days at Obidos; that the corps of Bacellar was descending along the Tagus; that already the peasants of Beira, led by the monks of Monsanto, had entered Abrantes, and had murdered there some sick soldiers, and that Pepin de Bellisle, the corregidor mor, had been treacherously assassinated. The intelligence from Lisbon was likewise alarming.

Under these disastrous circumstances, ought the army to try once more the fate of arms? If it ought, then, how? If it could not, what course was to be pursued?

Opinions were unanimous on the three questions. Enough had been done for the honour of the army. The troops were now no longer able to keep the field. To give battle to such numerous enemies, would be only leading the soldiers to the slaughter. Neither at Lisbon, nor in any other part of the kingdom, were there strong points, prepared and provisioned in such a way as to render it practicable to wait for the arrival of succours from France, at some tardy and uncertain future period. The evacuation of Portugal was, therefore, compulsory.

But to open a passage through the Peninsula, for the purpose of rejoining the French armies on the Ebro, even should the attempt be successful, must be a long and sanguinary task. Why, then, not endeavour to treat with the English on this basis, that, in exchange for Lisbon and the fortresses to be given up to them, they should convey the French army to France in their vessels? This proposition was reasonable; there was nothing in it which was derogatory to military honour, seeing that Lisbon, which it was thus intended to give up, could no longer contribute to our defence, and that the army was like a garrison that capitulates with the breaches open, and after having sustained two assaults. Yet even this was at first repugnant to the feelings of men who were unaccustomed to make this sort of composition with their enemies. It was, however, unanimously adopted. When, besides, it was taken into account that independent of the disastrous chances which would be avoided by negotiating, the advantage would also be gained of stipulating conditions, which might tend to preserve the fleet of the Russians, our allies, and to protect such Portuguese as had attached themselves to the French cause, and must remain in the country, these two additional considerations won over every suffrage. The general of division, Kellermann, was immediately despatched to the English head-quarters, and the army began its march to cover Lisbon.

The choice of the negotiator showed the issue which was expected for the negotiation. Kellermann bore a name which was known throughout Europe, in consequence of the ancient glory of his father, the conqueror of Valmy, and because he himself, leading the cavalry at Marengo, had decided, by a brilliant charge, the fortune of that immortal day. In him, the boldness of the warrior was united with the observant subtilty of the diplomatist. When he arrived at the English advanced posts, accompanied by a trumpeter and an interpreter, the utmost uneasiness was visible; the guards fired their muskets, and the regiments hastened to range themselves in battle. This involuntary movement of surprise and alarm showed him that the English army had not the confidence and security of victory. it was not Sir Harry Burrard that now commanded: Sir Hew Dalrymple, the definitive Commander-in-chief, had just landed. He could not conceal the satisfaction which he felt at seeing the French make overtures. Knowing neither the situation of the army nor of the country, he commissioned Sir Arthur Wellesley to confer with General Kellermann. The latter had, in conversation, carefully attended to those abrupt sentences, which, better than premeditated speeches expressed the thoughts and fears of the officers and chiefs. "The troops of Sir John Moore were still at a distance. It was doubtful whether so considerable a corps could he landed on so difficult a coast. The stormy weather hinders us from communicating with our transports. If it should last a little longer, we shall he starved. And what are the Portuguese doing? We can expect nothing from them."

Of these indiscretions General Kellerman took advantage, to talk largely of the resources and energy of the French, and especially of the great assistance they should derive from their allies, the crews of the Russian vessels. After a discussion of some hours, he concluded a preliminary arrangement and an armistice, of which the principal conditions were, —

That the French army should evacuate Portugal, and be conveyed by sea to France, with its artillery, arms, and baggage.

That the Portuguese, and the French established in Portugal, should not be molested for their political conduct, and that those who thought proper to depart, should he allowed a certain time to quit the country with their property.

That the Russian fleet should remain in the port of Lisbon as in a neutral port, and that whenever it sailed, it should not he pursued till the expiration of the term fixed by maritime law.

These conditions were to serve as the basis of a definitive treaty, to be settled by the Generals-in-chief of the two armies, and the British admiral, till which time there was to be a suspension of arms; the Sizandro forming the line of demarcation between the two camps, and the armed Portuguese not to advance beyond Leiria and Thomar. Forty-eight hours' notice was to be given previously to the renewal of hostilities between the armies of his Britannic Majesty, and those of his Imperial and Royal Majesty. The French negotiator took care to insert in the act the titles of his sovereign, precisely because the Cabinet of St. James's did not officially recognise the Emperor Napoleon. General Kellermann rejoined the French army on the 23rd, at Cabeça de Montachique, and, on the same day the General-in-chief re-entered Lisbon, at the head of the grenadiers and of his two regiments of cavalry.

It was high time for him to do so. The members and civil officers of the government, and particularly the numerous Portuguese who had espoused the French cause, were all in consternation. Some hid themselves, others sought refuge on board the fleet. The ministers assembled in the arsenal of the Fundiao, a large building by the seaside. The garrison of the castle had been transferred thither, to perform the police duty of the city. The ships of war were moored near the shore, in such a manner as, in case of revolt, to be able, on the one side, to sink the vessels with the prisoners, and, on the other, to sweep the quays, and the streets leading to the sea.

These precautions were quite necessary, for a population of two hundred thousand souls was boiling with hatred and hope. On the 20th, the combat of Roliça became known, and the inhabitants, spreading themselves in the Rocio, in Commerce Square, and in the lower part of the town, began to utter cries of fury against the French. The exertions of one good man were sufficient to disperse this tumultuous assemblage; this was General Travot. The Portuguese loved and honoured that officer, because he had not been employed in any expedition against the insurgents, and because, in his command at Oeyras, instead of oppressing the country, he had assisted the unfortunate with his purse and his advice. On this occasion he was not afraid to trust himself in the midst of the populace, accompanied by Brigadier general Frezier and some officers. He urged and intreated them to disperse. The calmness of his countenance made such an impression on them that they returned peaceably to their homes.

But as the danger was still imminent, General Travot thought it necessary to recall the thirty-first light battalion from Almada to Lisbon, though Setubal was occupied, and all the country overrun by the insurgents of the left bank of the Tagus. Then came the news of the action of Vimeiro, which the Intendant of the Police announced as a victory, while other information spoke of it as a defeat. On the 23rd, when troops were reported to be coming, many inhabitants of Lisbon went to meet them at the Campo Grande, uncertain whether it was English or French that they were going to see.

In the mean time, the arrangement of Vimeiro was merely temporary. Admiral Cotton refused to allow of the neutrality of the port of Lisbon for the Russians. During the eight months which he lad blockaded their squadron, he had not failed to consult his government as to the conduct which was to be observed towards them, in every possible case. He was ordered to detain the vessels, and send the crews back to Russia. Such were the instructions given by the Admiralty, even before an army had landed and been victorious in Portugal.

This first obstacle to the conclusion of a definitive convention gave rise to others which had not been foreseen. Instead of conferences taking place between the French General-in-chief and the commanders of the British land and sea forces, the negotiation was carried on at Lisbon, by General Kellermann and Lieutenant-colonel Murray, Quartermaster-general of the English army. Difficulties arose every moment: the negotiations were several times on the point of being broken off. The English General denounced, on the 28th of August, the rupture of the armistice, and the march of his army towards Lisbon. The Portuguese, under Bernardin Freire, moved forward to l'Incarnation, near Mafra. Bacellar's Portuguese corps was ordered to embark in boats at, and endeavour to surprise the Hanovenian legion at Sacavem.

JUNOT'S INVASION

The Count of Castro Marim, with six thousand men of the armies of Alemtejo and Algarve, marched from Evora towards the Tagus. Colonel Lopez blockaded Palmela, and occupied Setubal with bands of ferocious peasants, who murdered the French aid-de-camp, Marlier, whom General Graindorge had sent to them with a flag of truce. At the same time General Beresford arrived off the mouth of the Tagus from Cadiz, with the forty-second regiment. The eleven thousand men under Sir John Moore also landed at Maceira; and Admiral Cotton pressed Sir Hew Dalrymple to detach a part of his corps to Setubal, to join the Portuguese of Alemtejo, and cut off the retreat of the French to Elvas.

The firmness of Junot was still greater than the danger of his situation. He said to the Russians, "You have six thousand five hundred soldiers and sailors; you do not want more than a thousand for the duty of your ships while they are at anchor: form them into six large battalions. With this reinforcement, I will wait, either for succours from France, for the tempestuous season, or for a convention which will save my army and your squadron." To the English he said, "Take back your treaty, I am not in need of it; I will defend the streets of Lisbon inch by inch; I will burn all that I am obliged to leave to you, and you will see what it will cost you to win the rest."

So he would have done. Siniavin preferred treating separately with the English, and giving up his vessels to them, to running with the French a risk which might have insured glory and safety. The question as to the Russians being thus put aside, was a great step towards a definitive convention. That convention could be nothing more than a developement of the conditions clearly stipulated in the arrangement of Vimeiro, which arrangement was protected in the army by the military popularity of General Wellesley, by whom it was signed. Some modifications were agreed to by both parties, on account of the scarcity of transports. The number of artillery and cavalry horses, which the army was to take with it, was reduced to six hundred. It was also decided, that the French merchants established at Lisbon should not remove the merchandise which constituted their property, but only be allowed to dispose of it. All the other stipulations favourable to the French, and to the Portuguese who had taken part with them, were preserved, and even enlarged, in the definitive convention of evacuation, signed on the 30th of August, which is known by the name of Cintra, because the headquarters of the English army were at that place, when Sir Hew Dalrymple ratified it by affixing his seal.*

The name and authority of the Prince Regent of Portugal, and of the Supreme Junta which governed in his absence, were not mentioned in the Convention of Cintra. No thought was taken of claiming the Portuguese soldiers or sailors, or the deputies who were detained in France. The English generals dispensed with consulting, as to the treaty, those who had not assisted them to fight. All was settled without the participation of the Portuguese. They, however, loudly remonstrated. Bernardin Freire and the Count of Castro Marim formally protested against several articles of the convention, especially against that which, in contempt of the sovereignty of the Prince Regent, secured impunity and safety to all the partisans of the French. On the part of the inhabitants of Lisbon there arose accusations and murmurs, because they supposed the French army was going to carry off all the riches of the kingdom. Murmurs and accusations were, however, soon drowned in the obstreperous joy which the deliverance of their country excited in them.

A deeper impression was produced in England by the same event; there they were intoxicated with the success of the Spaniards, and not a doubt was felt that the army of Junot would at least experience a like fate with that of Dupont. The Convention of Cintra was received with such signs of indignation and grief as had never before been manifested, not even for the convention of Closter-Seyen, in the Seven Years' War, or, more recently, for the capitulations of the Helder and Buenos Ayres. The journalists surrounded their papers with black borders, in token of public mourning; and innumerable caricatures appeared, in which three gibbets were raised, for the three generals who had succeeded each other in the chief command. The Common Council of the city of London assembled constitutionally, and carried to the foot of the throne its complaints against an act which it declared to be "disgraceful to the British name, and injurious to the best interests of the British nation." Other political bodies, in the three kingdoms, spoke the same language. In compliance with this burst of public opinion, the Government was obliged to submit the convention of Cintra to a solemn enquiry.

This same public opinion, under the influence of a representative constitution, would not have allowed responsible ministers to violate a promise given, and drawn up in writing. The convention was faithfully executed, as far as depended on the English authorities. The French troops could not be immediately embarked, because the transports which were to convey them to France, the same that had brought the British troops to Portugal, had not their supply of provisions ready. The fortnight which the French now spent at Lisbon, was not the least difficult period of the occupation. The Portuguese insurgents arrived there in swarms, bedizened with feathers and ribands, wearing on their arms as many scarfs as they pretended to have killed enemies, and having their hats ornamented with the darling motto, *Death to the* French! Nothing was heard in the streets but crackers, musket and pistol firing, and sanguinary cries. The French army was encamped in the squares and on the heights, with batteries pointed towards the principal streets. Though its discipline overawed its enemies, yet the patrols were hourly attacked, and soldiers were assassinated. This state of things lasted till the middle of September, at which epoch the troops went on board, and the transports put to sea.

The garrisons of Elvas and Almeida did not arrive in time to embark with the army. As soon as the news of the convention of Cintra reached Badajoz, the Spaniards thought it a favourable opportunity to seize upon Elvas. General Galluzo, who commanded the army of Estremadura, summoned the fortress repeatedly. It had for its governor a firm and vigilant officer, Girod de

Novilars, chief of battalion of engineers, who treated the summonses with contempt. On the 7th of September, six thousand Spaniards arrived before Elvas, with a numerous train of field artillery. On the 9th, they completed the investment of the place. The governor evacuated the town, the defences of which had long been in ruins: he left a company in Fort Saint Lucia, and shut himself up, with the remainder of his garrison, in Fort la Lippe, which commands Elvas and the country. The Spaniards again summoned the governor, and meeting with no better success than before, opened a cannonade from the summit of the Serra de Maleffe. However, on the 20th of September, an English regiment arrived to take possession of the place. The governor then departed, taking with him not merely the garrison of Elvas, but also the French civil and military officers who had been detained for four months at Badajoz, and who were given up in consequence of an arrangement concluded at Lisbon, by General Kellermann, through the intervention of the English. The garrison of Elvas embarked, on the 17th of October, at Aldea Gallega, opposite Lisbon.

When Bacellar's corps descended into Lower Beira, he took with him all the troops of the line and the greatest part of the militia. There remained before Almeida only the second regiment of the militia of Guarda. This troop was posted in the village of Junea, a league from the place. A party of the garrison made a sally on the 15th of August, the Emperor's birthday, surprised the militia, killed several of them, and put the rest to flight. After this rout, the Portuguese contented themselves with watching Almeida at a distance, and falling upon straggling individuals, belonging to the weak detachments which were sent out from this place. A warlike monk, brother José de la Madre de Dios, poisoned, with a mixture of nux vomica and lime, some springs near the glacis, at which the soldiers occasionally quenched their thirst, and a tank, at which the cattle belonging to the garrison were watered.

Early in October, Almeida was given up to the English, in execution of the convention of Cintra, and the garrison was marched to Oporto, to be embarked there. The presence of fourteen hundred armed French occasioned a more violent riot than any that had occurred during the first scenes of the Portuguese restoration, More than fifteen thousand of the inhabitants of the town and country rushed upon the unfortunate soldiers, who were unable to defend themselves, even with the assistance of the two hundred English by whom they were escorted. They had only time to seek an asylum on board the English vessels in the river. The assailants embarked in boats, surrounded the ships, and tried to board them. The soldiers had only sixty cartridges per man for their defence. The bishop and the magistrates interposed. Their influence, however, would have been unavailing but for the presence of Sir Robert Wilson, colonel of a newly-levied Portuguese corps, called the Lusitanian Legion, which was then organising at Oporto, at the expense of England. This generous enemy succeeded, at the risk of his own life, in rescuing the luckless French from the rage of the people. But he could only save their lives. Disarmed and despoiled, the garrison of Almeida was conveyed by sea to the mouth of the Tagus. where, on the 18th of October, it rejoined the garrison of Elvas and a part of the eighty-sixth regiment, which had been separated from the convoy by a tempest, and forced to put back to Lisbon.

At the same period the army which had borne the name of the Army of Portugal, was disembarked on the French coast. The Duke of Abrantes landed at Rochelle, and, with him or after him, three thousand men. The rest of the army was conveyed to Quiberon, in pursuance of orders from the English Government, received during the passage. Quiberon and L'Orient being the points most distant from Spain, at which, according to the stipulations of the Convention of Cintra, the French could be put on shore. Quiberon was preferred, as offering more difficulties to the landing, and less resources for supplying the troops with provisions; thus delaying, as much as possible, their return to the Peninsula.

Twenty-nine thousand men had been sent into Portugal by the Emperor Napoleon; namely, twenty-five thousand with General Junot, and four thousand, who subsequently rejoined the regiments, from the hospitals and depôts. Three thousand perished, either of fatigue on the road from Bayonne to Lisbon, and in the marches during the burning summer of 1808, or assassinated individually by the Portuguese peasants, or of a natural death in the hospitals. Two thousand fell in the field of battle, or were made prisoners in various engagements. Two thousand of those who were embarked never arrived; one part of them being lost at sea, with the vessels which contained them, and the rest, who were Swiss, deserting to the English army. Twenty-two